D1616371

Chilton's

Repair and Tune-Up Guide

for the

VOLVO

Illustrated

Second Edition

PRODUCED BY THE AUTOMOTIVE BOOK DEPARTMENT

CHILTON BOOK COMPANY
PHILADELPHIA   NEW YORK   LONDON

Copyright © 1971 by Chilton Book Company.
Published in Philadelphia by Chilton Book Company,
and simultaneously in Ontario, Canada,
by Thomas Nelson & Sons, Ltd.
Second Edition   All rights reserved.
Manufactured in the United States of America.
ISBN   0-8019-5635-8
Library of Congress Catalog Card No. 73-146881

ACKNOWLEDGMENTS

Chilton Book Company expresses appreciation to these firms for their generous assistance:

ROBERT BOSCH CORPORATION
Long Island City, New York

CHAMPION SPARK PLUG COMPANY
Toledo, Ohio

THE GOODYEAR TIRE & RUBBER COMPANY
Akron, Ohio

Contents

Identification and Maintenance

The Volvo Story

The world's first production Volvo—an open touring car with a 28-bhp, four-cylinder engine—rolled off the assembly line in Gothenburg, April 14, 1927, heralding the beginning of the Swedish car company Aktiebolaget Volvo and climaxing the dreams of businessman Assar Gabrielsson and technician Gustaf Larsson.

It was only three years earlier that Gabrielsson and Larsson had set out to start a car company, but it must have seemed to them a lifetime. In 1924, there was a pall of depression on the market. The motor industry was entirely dominated by imported cars. Most observers prophesied quick failure for the Swedish car company, and nobody was willing to risk investing in the adventurous project. However, Gabrielsson and Larsson saw several factors favoring a car industry in Sweden. And so, to impress certain financiers, the two pioneers completed drawings for their future car and began manufacture with their own capital. Their system of assembling cars—building some

parts and procuring others from sub-suppliers (a few of whom now constitute the core of the AB Volvo Manufacturing Group)—gave rise to the expression, "building cars the Volvo way," which has followed Volvo through the years.

Gabrielsson and Larsson completed ten test vehicles, and the following year, in 1926, their efforts were rewarded: a far-sighted group—directors of the Swedish Ball Bearing Company (SKF)—invested large capital in the newly established company. They named it Volvo (Latin for "I roll") after a subsidiary of SKF. Within months, Volvo cars were being exported to several Scandinavian countries. But Volvo did not enter the U.S. market until 1956.

Early Volvos set the basic design for years to come. Then in 1944, a revolutionary car which had been designed during the war was introduced. This model, the PV 444/544 became one of Volvo's outstanding successes, paralleled only by the 1957 model 121/122S cars that have long topped Swedish registration statistics and dominated many of the export markets. The 122S in the U.S. in 1966 became the third best selling import sedan, demand

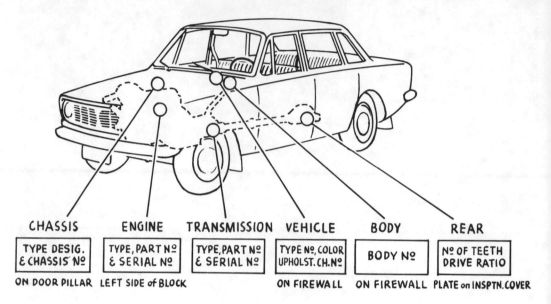

CHASSIS	ENGINE	TRANSMISSION	VEHICLE	BODY	REAR
TYPE DESIG. & CHASSIS N°	TYPE, PART N° & SERIAL N°	TYPE, PART N° & SERIAL N°	TYPE N°, COLOR UPHOLST. CH. N°	BODY N°	N° OF TEETH DRIVE RATIO
ON DOOR PILLAR	LEFT SIDE of BLOCK		ON FIREWALL	ON FIREWALL	PLATE on INSPTN. COVER

Series 144 vehicle identification.

exceeding the supply despite a price competitive to U.S. cars. The 122S is a two-door sedan with a 100 hp, twin-carb, 4-cylinder engine of 109 cubic inches.

Volvo's excellent materials and workmanship were never more manifest than in the Model 1800S GT sport coupe introduced in 1964. Also a 109 cubic inch engine, the 1800S offers good handling and a top speed of 110 mph. A five main bearing crankshaft is one of many extra design features. Clutch pedal pressure is reduced by a diaphragm type pressure spring rather than the usual coil springs.

In 1967, Volvo added a luxury, contemporary style four-door compact known as the 144S (two-door, 142S) with all the safety devices pioneered by Volvo over many years, such as padded interiors, disc brakes, collapsible steering wheel, shoulder lap seat belts, and doors that stay closed on impact. Volvo was first to offer shoulder lap seat belts, and they are standard equipment on these cars.

In 1968 the 140 line was supplemented with the addition of a station wagon, the Model 145S. More modern than the 122S station wagon, it includes all the luxuries and safety items of the 140 series. At the time of the introduction of the 145S, the

B18 engine was replaced with the two liter B20 engine.

In 1969, the Volvo line was again expanded by the introduction of the luxurious, powerful Model 164. This prestigious automobile is powered by a three liter, six cylinder engine. The B30 engine is a direct descendant of the thoroughly reliable B20 engine.

With 17 factories throughout the country, Volvo is Sweden's largest individual exporter. It is the second largest engineering concern in Scandinavia, exporting high quality products worldwide to more than 130 different markets.

How To Take Care of Your Volvo

Tools

This book contains the recommended Volvo tool number where applicable. It is not necessary to use only the Volvo tool, as many of the tools are fairly standard in any garage. For specialized service tools, see your Volvo dealer.

Model Identification

In all correspondence with the dealer or when ordering spare parts, the type designation, chassis number and engine number of the Volvo should be quoted for proper identification.

Type designation and chassis number are stamped on the cowl under the hood (on the right door column in the 144S and 164S). The type designation is also stamped on a plate to the left of this, with the code number for body color and upholstery. The engine type designation, part number and serial number are given on the left side of the cylinder block. Stamped on a tab are the last figures of the part number followed by the serial number. In identifying the engine, both the part number and serial number should be given.

Recommended Lubrication

Getting continuous top performance from fine machinery requires periodic maintenance using recommended lubricants.

Engine oil level is accurately shown on the dip stick only when the engine is warm but *not* running—preferably after sitting awhile to allow oil to drain into sump.

When flushing crankcase appears advisable, use the proper quantity of 10W oil (See table) and idle engine at 1000 rpm until oil is hot. Drain crankcase and filter immediately after stopping engine. Install new filter and recommended oil.

Engine Identification

Number of Cylinders	Displacement Cu. In. (cc)	Type	Model
4	86(1410)	OHV	B-14A
4	96.4(1580)	OHV	B-16A
4	96.4(1580)	OHV	B-16B
4	96.4(1580)	OHV	B-16D
4	109(1780)	OHV	B-18A
4	109(1780)	OHV	B-18B
4	109(1780)	OHV	B-18D
4	122(1990)	OHV	B-20A
4	122(1990)	OHV	B-20B
6	183(2980)	OHV	B-30A

Replacing oil filter every 6,000 miles requires care when tightening retaining nut. One-half turn beyond firm contact should adequately seal the gasket. Check for leaks after starting engine.

Vehicle Identification

Year	Model	Starting Chassis Number
1956	PV444	-
1957	PV444	-
1958	PV444	151123
1959	PV444	18501
1959	PV544	196005
1960	PV544	240387
1961	PV544	244000
1962	PV544/C	302360/330100
1963	PV544	334061
1964	PV544	369000
1965	PV544	406043
1966	PV544	427078
1959	122	21000
1960		28167
1961		29000
1962		55741
1963	(4 door)	87743
1963	(2 door)	2461
1964	(4 door)	112000
1964	(2 door)	11600
1965	(4 door)	150532
1965	(2 door)	57555
1966	(4 door—stick)	176814
1966	(4 door—automatic)	176822
1966	(2 door—stick)	108243
1966	(2 door—automatic)	108258
1966	(Station Wagon)	22217
1962	P1800	101
1963	P1800	326
1964	1800S	6001
1965	1800S	9247
1966	1800S	13679
1967	1800S	-
1968	1800S	-
1969	1800	-
1970	1800	-
1967	142	-
1968	142	-
1969	142	-
1970	142	-
1967	144	-
1968	144	-
1969	144	-
1970	144	-
1968	145	-
1969	145	-
1970	145	-
1969	164	-
1970	164	-

(The 122 rows from 1959 through 1966 are bracketed together and labeled "122")

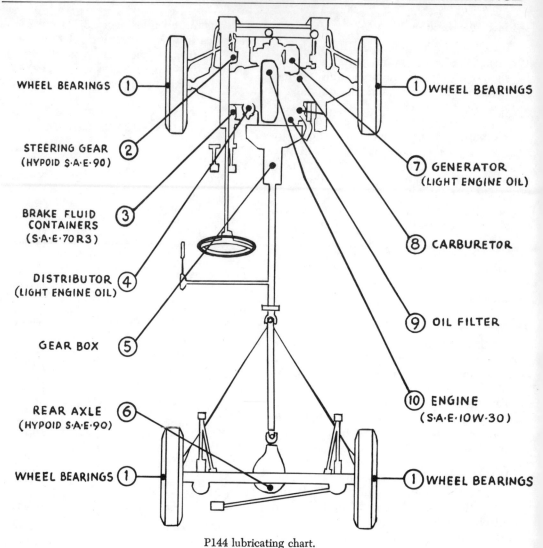

WHEEL BEARINGS ①   ① WHEEL BEARINGS

STEERING GEAR ②
(HYPOID S·A·E·90)

     ⑦ GENERATOR
        (LIGHT ENGINE OIL)

BRAKE FLUID ③
CONTAINERS
(S·A·E·70 R3)

     ⑧ CARBURETOR

DISTRIBUTOR ④
(LIGHT ENGINE OIL)

     ⑨ OIL FILTER

GEAR BOX ⑤

     ⑩ ENGINE
        (S·A·E·10W·30)

REAR AXLE ⑥
(HYPOID S·A·E·90)

WHEEL BEARINGS ①   ① WHEEL BEARINGS

P144 lubricating chart.

1. The wheel bearings are filled at the factory with a special type grease which covers the entire lifetime of the bearing. For this reason, it is not necessary to change or add lubricant. This also applies after reconditioning or changing of the bearings, provided that the bearings are then lubricated with a high-class grease.
2. Check that oil reaches up to the filler plug. Use hypoid oil SAE 80 all year round.
3. Check that the brake fluid reaches up to the Max mark. If necessary, add brake fluid which meets the requirements according to SAE 70 R 3.
4. Use light engine oil in the distributor.
5. Every 300 miles, check that the oil reaches up to the filler plug. Change oil after every 25,000 miles. Note: The quality of oil needed depends on the type of gearbox.
6. Every 3000 miles, check that the oil reaches up to the filler plug. Use hypoid SAE 90.
7. Fill the lubricating cap, if fitted, with light engine oil. The lubricating cap is opened by turning the outer cap. Use an ordinary can, not a force-feed type.
8. Check the oil level in the carburetor when changing the engine oil.
9. Change the oil filter every 6000 miles.
10. Check the oil level every time you buy gas.

Using oil of proper viscosity aids cold starting by increasing cranking speed.

Change transmission oil by removing drain plug at bottom of housing. Wipe area clean and remove filter plug. Fill overdrive transmissions with SAE 30 lubricant so that oil comes up to fill plug opening when car is level. Capacity is 3½ pints; 3 pints for the 164. Fill standard transmissions with SAE 90. Capacity 1½ pints. Capacity of automatic transmissions is 13¼ pints of Type A lubricant.

No lubrication fittings are provided on Volvos except on the clutch controls of B16 engines. All bearings and joints are either sealed and self lubricating or use

Engine Oil

Temperature Ranges	Viscosity
Above 90°F.	30W, SAE 10W-30
Above Freezing (+32° to 90°F.)	20W, SAE 10W-30
Between 0° and +32°F.	10W, SAE 10W-30
Below 0°F.°	5W, SAE 5W-20

° SAE 5W oil is not recommended for sustained high speed driving. SAE 5W-30 can also be used in this temperature range.

Note: When changing the oil during the Autumn and Winter seasons, consider the lowest anticipated temperature for the next 60 days.

materials not requiring lubrication.

Rear axle requires SAE 90 multipurpose gear lubricant. Capacity is 2.75 pints; 3⅓ for the 164.

Steering system oil ordinarily need not be changed. However, when the level is low, fill with SAE 90 lubricant. Capacity is ½ pint; 1⅓ for the 164.

Lubricate carburetor linkage at all pivot points with one or two drops of engine oil while moving throttle controls. Oil accelerator pump rods. Disconnect all ball joints, fill cups with high temperature grease or lubriplate and reconnect. Move linkage back and forth to check for proper functioning.

Check oil level in SU carburetor damping cylinders at every lubrication. Do not overfill. Use SAE 20 (not SAE 10-30) or automatic transmission fluid.

Lubricate distributor cam with non-corrosive high temperature grease. Re-move distributor cap, lift off the rotor and apply a thin coating to the cam. Do not allow grease or dirt to contaminate breaker points.

Hinges and locks of luggage compartment and doors should be lubricated every 6,000 miles or at least once a year to avoid squeaks and eliminate unnecessary wear. Use stick type graphite lubricant on door jamb strikers. Take an additional few minutes to clear door and body drain holes so that water cannot be trapped. In freezing weather, door and luggage compartment locks should be treated with a suitable lubricant to prevent them from freezing.

Maintenance Suggestions

The Appendix presents units of the metric system with the English equivalents, matching the precision of each to the nearest 1/100,000 .

However, the mechanic who becomes familiar with the metric system won't be troubled with looking up conversions to factory-issued metric specifications. Common metric sizes are not the common American sizes—finding American wrenches to fit an uncommon size is frequently difficult. The best preparation for working on any imported engine is to master the metric system and use a set of metric tools.

Because British terminology for European assemblies and components is most

Frequent Maintenance Checks

Engine Oil	Check level. Change every 6000 miles or 2 months with multi-grade oil, every 3000 miles or 2 months with single grade oil.
Battery Fluid	Check level. Add chemical-free drinking water. Do not overfill; neutralize spilled acid with baking soda and flush with clean water.
Engine Coolant	Check level. Note presence of sediment. Refill drained radiator with anti-freeze solution.
Lubrication	Hinges and locks; windshield wiper linkage; carburetor linkage.
Tires	Check pressure and wear.

6000-Mile Inspection and Maintenance

General

Leaks	Visual check for fuel, oil.
Fluid Levels	Transmission, rear axle, master brake cylinder.
Filters	Clean fuel pump strainers, sediment bowl, oil-damp air cleaner. Replace air filter cartridge, oil filter.
Lubrication	Wheel bearings, suspension parts, carburetor linkage, chassis fittings.

Electrical

Battery	Check condition of charge, clean cables.

Ignition

Spark Plugs	Inspect, clean or replace, set electrode gap.
Distributor	Lubricate cam, inspect and clean or replace points, reset.
Timing	Check timing and reset if necessary.

Carburetor

Fuel Flow	Check for proper jetting and atomization of fuel.
Idle Speed	Set idle speed.

Engine

Valve Clearance	Check against specifications and reset if necessary.
Crankcase	Inspect Positive Crankcase Ventilation valve.
Fan Belt	Inspect belt and correct the tension if necessary.
Compression	Test for equal compression in all cylinders.
Rocker Arm Shaft	Check tighteners.

Clutch

	Check pedal travel and free play.

Suspension

Control Arm Ball Joints	Check for wear.
Front Axle	Check for excessive play.

Wheels

Alignment	Tighten wheel nuts, correct balance, adjust alignment.
Brakes	Test for proper operation, fluid leaks, adequate pedal.
Pads and linings	Remove wheel and inspect. Measure wear.

Tires

	Rotate and check pressure.

often used in translations from German, it is advantageous to understand the British wording. If communication with European manufacturers ever becomes necessary, writing the British phraseology will prevent confusion and wrong deliveries. Some terms are given in the text in parentheses, and a more complete listing of British terms and American equivalents is in the Appendix.

BATTERY CARE

Volvos with B18 engines have used 12-volt batteries since 1962. Earlier B14 and B16 models were equipped with 6-volt systems. The Volvo 12-volt electrical system requires that the battery produce at least 9 volts while starter is cranking the engine. The 6-volt system can tolerate a minimum of 4.5 volts output under the cranking load.

Batteries should be checked periodically for proper output and good connections. A weak power supply lowers the efficiency of the engine and places a greater drag on the generator circuit.

Inspect the battery case for cracks and weakness. A leaky battery should be replaced. Check the density (specific gravity) of the battery electrolyte with a hydrometer. Readings from a fully charged battery will depend on the make but will fall in the range of 1.260 to 1.310 times as heavy as pure water at 80°F. NOTE: *all cells should produce nearly equal readings*. If one or two cell readings are sharply lower, the cells are defective, and if readings continue to be low after charging, the battery must be replaced. (See Battery Replacement—Chapter 5).

As a battery releases its charge, sulphate ions in the electrolyte become attached to the battery plates—reducing the density of the fluid. The specific gravity of the electrolyte varies not only with the percentage of acid in the liquid, but also with temperature. As temperature increases, the electrolyte expands so that specific gravity is reduced in this second way. As temperature drops, the electrolyte contracts and gravity increases. To correct readings for temperature variations, add .004 to the hydrometer reading for every 10°F. that the electrolyte is above 80°F. and subtract .004 for every 10°F. that the electrolyte is below 80°F. The drawing shows the total correction to make for any temperature above or below 80°F.

The amount of charge remaining in a battery can be roughly determined from the specific gravity ranges shown in the chart below.

Hydrometer Readings	Condition
1.260–1.310	Fully charged
1.230–1.250	¾ charged
1.200–1.220	½ charged
1.170–1.190	¼ charged
1.140–1.160	Almost discharged
1.110–1.130	Fully discharged

Perform a light-load voltage test to detect weak cells. First draw off the transient (surface) charge by operating the starter for three seconds and then turning on the low beam lights. After one minute, test each cell (with lights still on) with a voltmeter. A fully charged battery will have no cell voltage below 1.95 volts and no cell should vary more than .05 volts from the others. A greater variation at full charge indicates a defective cell.

Another battery check involves connecting a charger for three minutes under 40

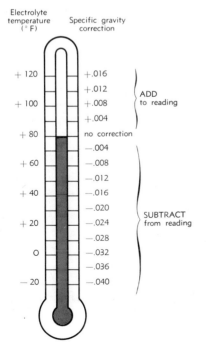

Temperature affects the specific gravity readings of batteries.

amperes for a 12-volt battery (75 amps for 6-v). Read the battery voltage with the charger still operating. Voltage over 15.5 v for 12-volt battery (7.75 for 6 v) indicates a defective battery. If battery voltage is under this limit and individual cell readings are within 0.1 volts the battery is usable.

Charging a weak battery is best done by a slow-charge method. If quick charging is attempted, check the cell voltages and the color of the electrolyte a few minutes after charge is started. If cell voltages are not uniform or if electrolyte is discolored with brown sediment, quick charging should be stopped in favor of a slow charge. In either case, do not let electrolyte temperature exceed 120°F.

If high electrical circuit voltage is suspected, the voltage regulator might be cutting in abnormally due to corroded or loose battery connections. The symptoms are hard starting, full ammeter charge and lights flaring brightly. After cleaning, coat battery terminals with petroleum jelly (vaseline) to prevent recurrence of problem.

Overcharging the battery is a common cause of battery failure. A symptom of overcharging is a frequent need for addition of water to the battery. The generating system should be corrected immediately to prevent internal battery damage.

COOLING SYSTEM

The engine is cooled by a pressurized system with a capacity of 9 quarts for the four cylinder engines and 13 quarts for the six. A double acting thermostat, with an opening temperature of 169°F. for the B18 and 179°F. for the B20 and B30, speeds up heating of the engine and assures optimum temperature under all operating conditions. The coolant level should be checked at each refueling.

Replace radiator coolant once a year, when the entire cooling system should be flushed clean with water. The recommended coolant is a mixture consisting of 40% ethylene glycol (Volvo Part No. 297176) and 60% water. To drain the cooling system, open the drain cock on the engine and remove the plug at the bottom of the radiator. Remove the expansion tank and empty its contents into the radiator.

Capacities and Pressures

Engine Model	Crankcase Capacity w/o filter (with filter) Pints	Crankcase Viscosity SAE	Transmission Cap. Pints	Transmission Vis-cosity SAE	Rear Axle Cap. Pints	Rear Axle Vis-cosity SAE	Fuel Tank Cap. Gals.	Fuel Fuel Pump Press. PSI	Cooling System Cap. with Heater Qts.	Cooling System Therm. Opens °F.
B14	7 (7.75)	10W-30					9.3	2 to 3		
B16A	6 (7)	10W-30					9.3	2 to 3.5	9.5	
B16B	6 (7)	10W-30	2	90	2		9.3	2 to 3.5	9	169
B18A	7 (8)	10W-30	1.5	90	2.75	90	11.8	1.5 to 3.5	9	169
B18B	7 (8)	10W-30	1.5	90	2.75	90	11.8	1.5 to 3.5	9	169
B18D	7 (8)	10W-30	1.5	90	2.75	90		1.5 to 3.5	9	169
B20	7 (8)	10W-30	1.6	90	2.75	90		1.5 to 3.5	9	169
B30	11 (12.7)	10W-30	1.3	90	3.4	90		2.1 to 3.5	13	179

Notes: 1. Overdrive transmission requires 3.4 pints SAE 30.
2. Automatic transmissions require 13.25 pints type A oil.

When refilling, the heater control must be set at "Max" heat so that the entire system can be filled. Fill the radiator to the top and put on the cap. Then fill the expansion tank to the "Max" mark or just above. Warm the engine and then check to make sure that the radiator is completely full and that the level lies between the marks on the expansion tank.

Effective cooling system protection against rust requires at least a 25% solution of the recommended antifreeze (+10°F.) through summer and winter. If water only is used, a water pump lubricant and a heavy duty cooling system protector should be added. Methanol or alcohol alone are not recommended for the Volvo cooling system. These agents with their low boiling points evaporate (boil off) in a short time. Ethylene glycol antifreeze compounds have boiling points close to 400°F., well above the heat range of water cooled engines. Anti-rust and lubrication additives are helpful in lubricating the water pump and protecting metal parts. The rust and foam inhibitors used in antifreeze lose their power with aging, particularly in older engines, with greater rust deposits. Antifreeze, itself, eventually loses its protective properties and becomes an irritant to the cooling system. Replace at the recommended intervals.

Antifreeze is harmful to the oil system of the engine. If cooling system fluid has leaked into the engine oil, ethylene-glycol-monobutyl-cellusolve, available from jobbers, is recommended for flushing the system.

Water condensation in the engine is often caused by limited use of the car. If an engine runs only two or three miles before being shut down, it does not maintain its proper operating temperature long enough to evaporate water that may be present in the crankcase. Regular oil changes will help eliminate water accumulation. Also check the thermostat for too-quick opening. If necessary, change the thermostat for hotter engine operation.

FAN BELT ADJUSTMENT

A tight fan belt will cause rapid wear of the generator and water pump bearings. A loose fan belt will slip and wear excessively, causing noise, engine overheating and fluctuating generator output. Fan belt tension is correct when light finger pressure deflects the belt one-half inch, or when a pull of 17 to 24 lbs. (8-11 kg) is required to slide the pulley. To measure this, pull the fan in the direction of engine rotation with a spring balance attached to one of the four blades at a point six inches out from the fan hub. An oily or frayed fan belt should be re-

Clutch Specifications

	B16 Engine in. (mm)	B18 Engine in. (mm)	B20 Engine in. (mm)	B30 Engine in. (mm)
Clutch Pedal Free Travel	.37"–.59" (10–15)	.37"–.59" (10–15)	.37"–.59" (10–15)	.37"–.59" (10–15)
Clutch Yoke Free Travel	.12" (3)	.12" (3)	.12" (3)	.12" (3)
Type	Single dry plate disc	Single dry plate disc	Single dry plate disc	Single dry plate disc
Size	8" (203)	8.5" (215.9)	8.5" (215.9)	9"
Pedal-Actuated Control	Mechanical	Hydraulic	Mechanical ①	Mechanical ①
Total Friction Area	52.7 sq. in. (340)[2]	68 sq. in. (440)[2]	68.2 sq. in. (440)[2]	72.5 sq. in. (468)[2]
Installed Plate Thickness	.28"–.29" (7–7.5)	.28"–.29" (7–7.5)		
Number and Size of Rivets	16; .14" x .25" (3.5 x 6.5)	16; .14" x .21" (3.5 x 5.5)	16; .14" x .21" (3.5 x 5.5)	
Number of Springs; length, loaded under 188–199 lb. (85.5–90.5 kg)	6; 1.5" (38)	6; 1.5" (38)		
Distance between Flywheel and Contact Surface of Clutch Levers with Throw-out Bearing	1.81" (46)	1.81" (46)		
Adjustment of Clutch Levers:		Alternative 1: .29" (7.5) below adjusting jig hub (SVO2065) within ±.06" (1.5) and within .01" (.25) of each other.	Adjustment 41.5" in clutch fixture SVO2322 with packing blocks No. O.	Alternative 2: Adjustment 40.5" in clutch fixture SVO2322 with packing blocks No. O.

① Right-hand steering and 1800S - hydraulic control.

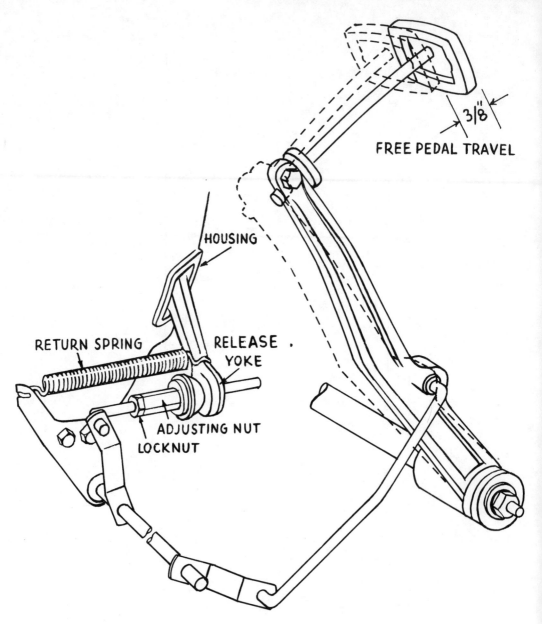

3/8"

FREE PEDAL TRAVEL

HOUSING

RETURN SPRING

RELEASE
YOKE

ADJUSTING NUT

LOCKNUT

Clutch adjustment, PV544, P210.

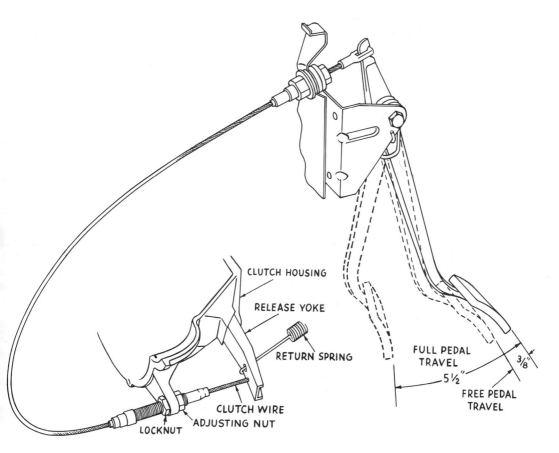

Clutch adjustment, 144.

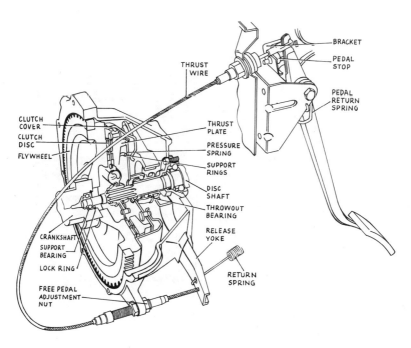

Clutch and clutch controls, 144.

placed. Remove the belt by loosening the generator mount. Tension the new belt by properly positioning the generator. Then tighten the mounting.

CRANKCASE VENTILATION

A positive crankcase ventilation system connects the crankcase with the intake manifold on the engine to return crankcase gases and exhaust blow-by to the combustion chambers for more complete burning. The system consists of an oil trap attached to the valve inspection cover on the right side of the engine (viewed from front) and two rubber hoses between which there is a control valve.

Every 25,000 miles, the hoses, fittings and valve should be cleaned, inspected and replaced if necessary.

AIR CLEANER MAINTENANCE

Replace paper filter element on the B18 engine every 12,000 miles under normal driving conditions and more frequently in severe environments. On B20 and B30 engines, replace the insert every 25,000 miles under normal conditions. In dusty or heavily polluted areas replace the insert more often. Do not moisten or oil paper elements. Engines use tons of air even at idle; restriction of air flow inevitably affects engine performance and increases fuel consumption.

Oil-damp type air filters should be washed in solvent, blown dry, and dampened again with oil. Clean every 6,000 miles.

CLUTCH PEDAL ADJUSTMENT

All Volvo gear shift models use single dry plate disc type clutches of Borg and Beck manufacture. Clutch control, actuated by the foot pedal, is hydraulic on 122S and 1800S models, mechanical on 164, 144, PV444, 445, 544 and P210 models. The required thrust on the pressure plate is provided by six strong pressure springs on all models except the 164 and 140 which utilize a diaphragm type spring.

Using a short set wrench loosen the locknut, and screw the adjusting nut until free pedal travel is ⅜″ to $^{19}\!/_{32}$″ (10-15 mm) and the release yoke has a travel of about ⅛″ to the ball on the clutch wire. Lock the adjusting nut with the locknut after ad-

justment is reached. Clutch pedal travel should be 5½″ (140 mm).

BRAKE CHECK AND ADJUSTMENT

Check condition of drum brakes by depressing pedal firmly. If pedal travels to within 2 inches of floor mat and has a hard feel, brake shoes require adjustment or relining. Remove wheel, hub and drum assembly to check lining. If worn nearly to rivets, reline brakes. If pedal has a spongy feel, brake system needs bleeding. Check fluid level in master cylinder reservoir and add fluid if necessary. Adjust drum type brakes by jacking up the car so the wheels are free to turn. Release the handbrake. Remove the rubber seal. Turn the wheel in a forward direction of rotation while turning the notched adjuster screw with a screwdriver inserted through the slot in

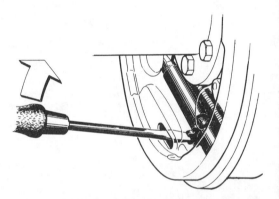

Using screwdriver to adjust brakes.

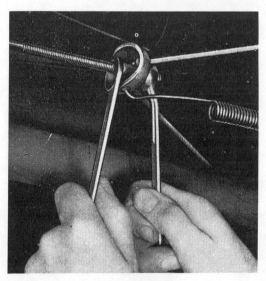

Adjusting handbrake.

the back plate. When the wheel can just be turned using one hand, back off the adjuster screw about 12 notches. Install the rubber seal.

Disc brakes do not require adjustment. However, the friction pads in the calipers must be checked for wear every 6000 miles. Brake pads should be replaced when 1⁄16″ or less lining remains.

Adjust parking brake when hand lever has a travel greater than ratchet clicks. Fully release hand lever, check cable freedom and loosen equalizer and adjusting nut. Pull lever up three clicks and tighten cable with rear brakes just beginning to bind. Check for equal action at both brakes. Lubricate cable.

FUSES

The fuse block is located either on the left front under the hood or on the heater element below the dash. If an electrical circuit blows a fuse, a new fuse should be installed after the cause of the trouble has been eliminated. A few spare fuses of the correct rating are good protection in emergencies.

Wheel and Tire Care

Wheel and Tire Balance

Wheel and tire balance is more critical with respect to tire wear than casual drivers realize. Unbalance is the principal cause of tramp, car shake, pounding and riding roughness. It often contributes to steering misalignment and damage.

Original balance of the tire and wheel is gradually lost as the tires wear. Severe acceleration, braking, cornering and side-slipping upset wheel balance in even less

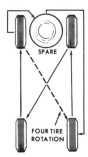

Broken line shows tire rotation pattern when not using spare.

Excessive wear along tire edges was caused by prolonged underinflation.

Excessive wear along center of tire tread was caused by prolonged overinflation.

Improper camber caused tire to wear on one side.

Abnormal wear across entire tread surface is a result of front end misalignment. If tread design wears in spots, the wheel is most likely out of balance.

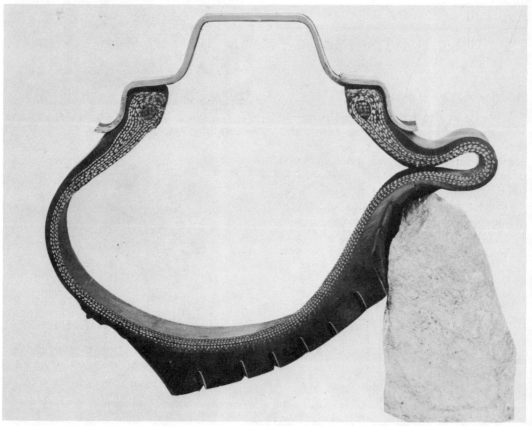

Bruise damage occurs from striking a rock or curb, particularly if the blow is to the sidewall area.

A simple test for tread life. If the head of the figure is partially covered, there is sufficient tread remaining for safety. Tires should be replaced if, as shown, coin can hardly be inserted in groove.

time. Wheels also need balancing after punctures are repaired.

Check wheel balance each time the tires are rotated—every 6000 miles—for maximum tire and front end life.

Tire Wear and Storage Notes

Tread design is one of the more important considerations in tire performance. The design affects acceleration, speed, cornering, braking, heat dissipation, wear, noise and related factors. Necessarily, tread pattern should be checked periodically for premature wear to a dangerous point.

Check tread life by placing a penny in a tread groove. If the top of Lincoln's head is completely exposed, the tire should be replaced or recapped. Ninety percent of tire failure occurs in the last 10% of tread life. A more convenient tread wear indicator is the solid crossbars of rubber that show across the tire when the tread pattern has worn to $\frac{1}{16}''$ of an inch. These bars are now required by Federal legislation for all tires.

STORAGE TIPS

To avoid shortening service life, tires must be properly stored while they are not in use. These tips will help keep stored tires in good condition.

1. Check the tires for road damage. Remove stones and other objects that may be trapped in the tread grooves. Have any necessary repairs made.

2. Store the tires in a clean, dry, cool, closed and dark room.

3. Keep the tires away from water, petroleum products such as gasoline and oil, electric motors and heat sources.

4. Place the tires on their sidewalls on a flat surface; permanent flat-spotting can result if the tires are stored standing on their treads.

5. Inflation pressure should be reduced to 12 to 16 pounds if tires are to be stored mounted on wheels.

6. White sidewall tires should be placed whitewall to whitewall, one on top of the other, to protect the white rubber from scuffs and dirt.

Tire Sizes and Pressures

Model	Inflation Pressure (PSI)			Rim Cross-sec. (in.)	Tire Size
	Normal Load		Heavy Loads Rear		
	Front	Rear			
122, 122S	21	23	28	4	5.90 x 15
PV444	18	21	26		—
PV544	20	23	26	4	6.00 x 15
P1800,					6.85 x 15 or
1800S	26	28			165SR-15
142, 144,				4.5	6.00 x 15 or
145					165-15
164				4.5	6.85 x 15 or
					165SR-15

General Dimensions

Model	Overall Dimensions (in.)			Ground Clear-ance	Weight (lbs.)
	Length	Width	Height		
164	186	68.3	56.7	7.0	2992
145	182.7	68.3	56.7	8.3	2702
144, 142	182.7	68.3	57.0	8.3	2600
1800	173.25	66.9			2460
145S	181	68.3	57.0	8.3	
144, 142	182.7	68.3	56.7	6.3	2640
1800S	173.25	66.9			2460
PV-544C	175	62.5	61.5	7.5	
122S	175	63.5	59.2	7.7	2366
P-1800	173	67	51	5.3	2430
122	175	63.5	59.2	7.7	2366
PV-544	175	62.5	61.5	7.5	

Chapter 2
Troubleshooting Checks

Locating No-Start Problems

When the cause of the engine failure is uncertain, the most efficient way to get the engine running smoothly again is to follow a series of troubleshooting checks that break no-start problems into four areas—engine-cranking, ignition, fuel and compression. Locating the no-start trouble is easily done by following this simple sequence.

1. First try to crank the engine with the starter. Slow engine cranking, or none at all, indicates that the trouble is in the battery, cables, switches or starter. Detailed testing to find the specific defect is provided in the next section of this chapter, *Testing No-Start Components*, ENGINE CRANKING SYSTEM CHECKS.

2. If engine-cranking checked out normal, disconnect a wire from a spark plug, hold it (avoid shock by wearing glove) about ¼ to ½-inch from the plug terminal, and have the engine cranked over with the ignition switched on. Check for strong, evenly timed arcs. The ignition system must supply (often through worn parts)

an amount of voltage necessary to form a bright spark at the electrode gap. If there is no spark or if the arc pulse is irregular or weak, the problem is in the ignition system. Special testing to identify ignition malfunctions is described in the next section, under IGNITION.

3. With cranking and ignition successfully checked, remove the air cleaner for access to the carburetor(s). Work the throttle linkage up and down. A stream of fuel should spurt from the accelerator jet(s). If no fuel ejects into the carburetor throat(s) after repeated throttle pumping, there is a defect in the fuel system. A less-common malfunction is continuous flooding of the carburetor(s). If the carb throats are soaked with gasoline and fumes are profuse, have the motor cranked and check for fuel streaming from the main jet(s) into the intake manifold. This check reveals another type of fuel system trouble. Extensive testing procedures are presented in the next section, under FUEL.

4. The last no-start troubleshooting check is for an infrequent, yet sometimes elusive problem—no compression. In most cases, compression failures show up in one

or two cylinders, and are normally not severe enough to prevent starting. However, having no compression in all cylinders will prevent starting. Complete compression failures can be caused by a jumped timing chain, a burnt valve, a broken camshaft, or possibly, the improper mating of timing gears in a newly rebuilt engine. Check for compression by removing a spark plug, sealing the piston chamber with a thumb, cork or other object, and having the engine cranked over. Good compression will gently pop the thumb from the opening. No-compression troubles are analyzed in another section, *Hard Starting, Poor Performance—Tuning.*

Testing No-Start Components

Once the no-start problem has been localized to one of the areas—engine-cranking, ignition, fuel, compression—special testing within that area can directly identify the malfunction while saving expense and valuable time. Each of the units below has a step-by-step troubleshooting test procedure to eliminate suspicion of working parts and to determine the exact trouble.

Engine Cranking System Checks

The engine-cranking network includes the battery, cables, switches and starter. The battery and cables are checked first because they are the storehouse and supply of all electrical power . . . . feeding

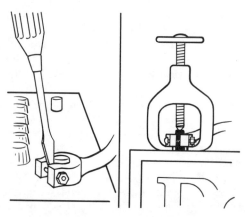

Spreading cable clamp and pulling it from battery terminal.

the starter motor, ignition system, lights, and accessories.

Turn on the headlights and crank the engine with the starter. If the lights dim out sharply and the cranking slows drastically, either the battery cables are making poor contact or the battery itself is nearly discharged.

If the headlights stay bright but the starter turns slowly or does not turn over, the starter cables or switches may be faulty or the starter defective. Check the difference in voltage readings taken at the battery and at the starter while the starter is cranking the engine to determine the voltage drop through the cables and solenoid.

CHECKING CABLES

Check the connections by carefully working a screwdriver between each cable connector and its terminal post. WARNING: *Hammering, jarring or prying against the terminal may loosen and short-out the battery plates.* If engine cranking improves, the trouble is the connection. Sometimes an imperfect connection can be identified simply by "smoke" or vapor rising from corrosion in that area when the starter switch is actuated.

Cleaning cables and terminals should be done with utmost care to prevent damage to the battery. If a cable cannot be removed by hand easily after the clamp bolt is loosened, a small screw-type puller should be used.

Thorough wire brushing or application of a strong baking soda solution will successfully clean terminals and connectors. CAUTION: *cleaning solution will damage the battery cells if allowed to seep through the vented caps.*

BATTERY TEST

If engine fails to crank after checking out the cable connections, the battery is discharged. A hydrometer reading can quickly tell if any cells are dead. A battery that is normal (though discharged) will have nearly equal specific gravity readings for each cell. (Readings of a fully charged battery range from 1.280 to 1.310, depending on the make.) But if one or two cells have a reading far lower than the others, there is an electrical short circuit within the battery. Tips for charging batteries prop-

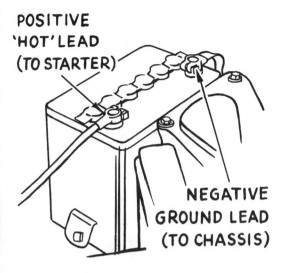

POSITIVE 'HOT' LEAD (TO STARTER)

NEGATIVE GROUND LEAD (TO CHASSIS)

Battery connections.

erly are given in Chapter I under Battery Care.

Once it has been determined that the battery is discharged, the generator and regulator must be checked for the proper charging rate. The electrical system is investigated in Chapter 5.

Testing Generator and Regulator

After checking condition and tension of fan belt, turn off all accessories, set engine speed up to around 2500 rpm, and attach ammeter in series with regulator and battery by disconnecting red lead from "B+" regulator terminal and adding ammeter between terminal and red wire. Output must be 20 amperes minimum on a 12-volt generator and 50 amperes on a 6-volt D.C. unit (at 2000 rpm). A lower

Electrical Specifications

Engine	Battery			Starter					Brush Spring Tension (lbs.)
	Capacity (amp. hrs.)	Voltage (volts)	Grounded Terminal	Lock Test		No Load Test			
				Amps	Volts	Amps	Volts	RPM	
B-14, B-16	85	6	Neg	450-500	3.5	60-80	5.5	4,000-5,000	1.75-2.00
B-18, B-20, B-30	60	12	Neg	300-350	6	40-50	12	6,900-8,100	2.53-2.86

Engine	Generator				Regulator				
	Part Number	Brush Spring Pressure (lbs.)	Field Resistance (ohms)	Max. Output (amps)	Part Number	Cut-out Relay		Max. Current (amps)	Voltage Regulator Setting (volts)
						Cuts in at (volts)	Reverse Current at (amps)		
B-18	Bosch LJ/ GG240/12/ 2400/AR6 or 7	1.0-1.3	4.8±0.5	30	Bosch RS/ VA240/12/ 12	12.4-13.1	2.0-7.5	45 cold 30 warm	14.1-14.8 idling, 13.0-14.0 loaded

Engine	Alternator			Regulator	
	Part Number	Output (amps) at rpm	Minimum Brush Length (in.)	Part Number	Voltage (volts) at alt. rpm, cold
B-20	Bosch K1(R)- 14V, 35A20	35 @ 1,200	.32	Bosch AD-14V	14.0-15.0 @ 4,000
B-30	S.E.V. Motorola 14V-26641	30 @ 1,500	.20	S.E.V. Motorola 14V-33525	13.1-14.4 cold, 13.85-14.25 hot

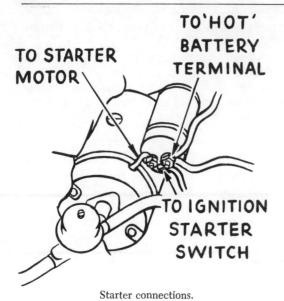

Starter connections.

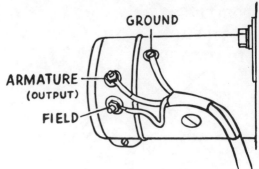

Generator connections.

output indicates malfunction in the generator or regulator. Identify the cause by disconnecting the generator field lead from the regulator and connecting it to the generator armature terminal. If output is still low, generator is faulty. Replace as in Chapter Five. If not, continue tests.

Remove red battery lead from regulator "B+" terminal and connect voltmeter positive lead to this terminal. Run voltmeter negative lead to ground. Increase engine speed until voltage peaks within 13.5–14.5 range. Six-volt regulator limits voltage to 7.0–7.5 volts.

If voltage reading is not in range, remove regulator cover and adjust voltage regulator armature spring tension to obtain a middle reading of 14.0 volts. If reading fluctuates, voltage contacts are dirty.

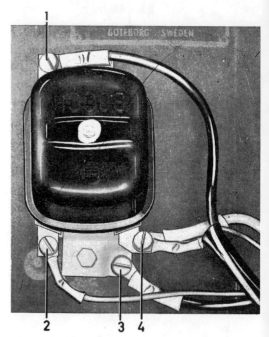

1. B+, to battery "hot" terminal
2. DF, to generator field
3. Ground
4. D+, to generator armature

Regulator connections.

Cutout Relay Closing Voltage— DC Regulator

Connect voltmeter positive lead to regulator "61" (lower rear) terminal. Attach negative lead to ground. Connect ammeter in series with "B+" (upper rear) terminal and disconnect red wire to battery. Increase engine speed and observe voltage increase (until cutout relay points close) and then drop slightly as circuit is completed to battery. The highest voltmeter reading before the drop is the closing voltage. Closing voltage: 12.3–13.2 volts; 5.9 to 6.5 volts. If closing voltage is

not within limits, adjust closing voltage by bending cutout relay spring support. Increase spring tension to increase closing voltage—decrease spring tension to decrease closing voltage.

Generator and regulator removal and repair are described in Chapter Five.

Testing the Alternator and Regulator

Bosch—Alternator Test

Connect the alternator as shown in the test diagram and run the engine at 1000

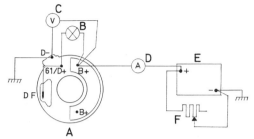

A. Alternator
B. Control lamp, 12 volts, 2 watts
C. Voltmeter, 0–20 volts
D. Ammeter, 0–50 amps
E. Battery
F. Load resistance

Wiring diagram for testing Bosch alternator.

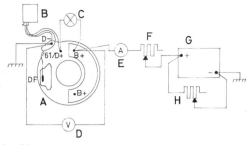

A. Alternator
B. Voltage regulator
C. Control lamp, 12 volts, 2 watts
D. Voltmeter, 0–20 volts
E. Ammeter, 0–50 amps
F. Control resistance
G. Battery
H. Load resistance

Wiring diagram for testing Bosch AC voltage regulator.

rpm, until the alternator is warm (about 140°F). It should then produce at least 23 amps at 14 volts. Adjust the voltage by means of the load resistance. Increase engine speed to 2000 rpm and check that the test and warning lights do not light. If the alternator does not meet the above specifications, check the brush holder and diodes.

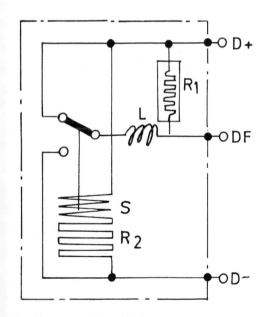

S—Voltage winding, 35 ohms
R₁—Regulator resistance, 2.45 ohms
R₂—Compensation resistance, 50 ohms
L—Contact impedence coil

Inner wiring of Bosch AC voltage regulator.

Bosch—Voltage Regulator Test

Connect the voltage regulator as shown in the test diagram and run the engine at 2000 rpm. Load the alternator with 28 to 30 amps. Lower the engine speed to idle, raise it again to 2000 rpm and adjust the load to 28 to 30 amps. The voltage should now be 14 to 15 volts. Adjustments should be made on the left (lower) contact.

Reduce the load to 3 to 8 amps. The voltage should now be between minus 0.9 and plus 0.2 volts of the first reading.

Lower range adjustments are made by bending the stop clamp. Bending up raises the voltage and bending down lowers the voltage.

Motorola—Voltage Drop Test

With a 10 amp load (headlights, for instance) the voltage drop between the B+ pole of the alternator and the positive pole of the battery should be less than 0.3 volts, and between the D— pole of the alternator and the negative pole of the battery should be less than 0.2 volts. If there is a greater drop, check the wiring and the ground connection.

Alternator Test

Connect the alternator as shown in the test diagram. Check that the current through the field is 2 to 2.5 amps. With the engine running at 1400 rpm, the alternator should deliver at least 30 amps at about 13 volts. Compare the voltage at the B+ pole

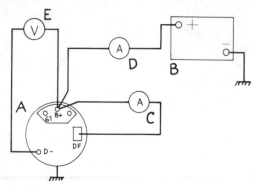

A. Alternator
B. Battery
C. Ammeter, 0–10 amps
D. Ammeter, 0–50 amps
E. Voltmeter, 0–20 volts

Wiring diagram for testing Motorola alternator.

and terminal 61. Voltage should be 0.8 to 0.9 volts higher at terminal 61, otherwise the isolation diode is faulty.

Voltage Regulator Test

Connect the voltage regulator as shown in test diagram. Run the engine at 2300 rpm for 15 seconds. The voltage at the voltmeter should be 13.1 to 14.4 volts with the alternator at 75°F (25°C).

Switch on the headlights (to give a load of about 10 to 15 amps). The voltage should be between 13.1 and 14.4 volts at about 75°F (25°C). If the voltage exceeds the tolerances, the voltage regulator should be replaced.

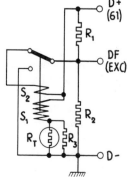

S₁ Voltage winding
S₂ Accelerator winding
R₁ Regulator resistance, 10 ohms ± 10%
R₂ Damper resistance, 30 ohms ± 10%
R₃ Compensation resistance (adapted to RT during manufacture)
RT Compensation thermistor, approximately 4 ohms at 75° F. (25° C.)

Motorola AC voltage regulator inner circuit.

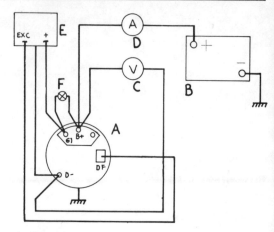

A. Alternator
B. Battery
C. Voltmeter, 0–20 volts
D. Ammeter, 0–50 amps
E. Voltage regulator
F. Test light, 12 volts, 2 watts

Wiring diagram for testing Motorola AC voltage regulator.

Checking Switches

After the battery and cables have been checked, the starting system switches should be tested.

(Test 1) First, bypass the starter switch by running a jump cable or other heavy-gauge lead directly from the positive terminal of the fully charged battery to the input terminal of the solenoid. (DANGER: Rings, watches and other metal in contact with the hand can cause severe burns with accidental battery-voltage contact. A heavy-cloth glove offers good protection against burns caused by sudden overheating of the jump cable.) If the starter motor comes to life when the electrical contact is made, the malfunction is in the starter switch or its wiring. If there is no starter response or just a click in the solenoid, make a second test.

(Test 2) Cautiously touch the hot cable directly to the starting motor input lead. This bypasses the solenoid. In a clutch-type starter assembly, the starter should spin but will not engage the flywheel when the solenoid is omitted from the circuit. If the starter spins, the trouble is in the solenoid unless the solenoid had clicked in the previous test. The solenoid serves two simultaneous functions—switching power into the starting motor and engaging the starter-clutch assembly. If the

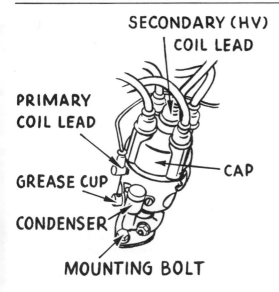

SECONDARY (HV)
COIL LEAD

PRIMARY
COIL LEAD

GREASE CUP

CAP

CONDENSER

MOUNTING BOLT

Distributor components.

solenoid clicked in the first test and the starting motor spun free in the second test, the solenoid is good and the trouble is a locked or frozen engine. (If starter gear is jammed against flywheel, place transmission in high gear and gently rock car back and forth.) Getting no response with the hot lead on the starter terminal indicates that the problem is in the starting motor itself.

STARTER CHECK

The intensity of the spark at the contact of the hot cable with the starter input may help determine the fault in the motor. A bright, nearly-welding flash indicates that there is a shorted circuit within the starting motor. A weak spark or none at all points to a poor connection of the motor brushes with the commutator. The brushes could be completely worn. The brush springs could be broken. The commutator could have burnt spots or be dirty or oily.

Chapter 5 provides detailed overhaul procedures for electrical equipment as well as procedures for testing assemblies with a voltmeter.

Ignition

Troubleshooting the ignition system for a no-start problem involves checking through the primary and secondary ignition circuits from the battery to the spark

plugs. Locating the shorted circuit can be done quickly by following the easy tests below.

The initial test for troubleshooting the ignition system was to check for the strength and pulse of the arc between a disconnected spark plug wire to its terminal ¼ to ½-inch away. A poor spark indicated ignition system trouble. (Locating No-Start Problems)

TESTING IGNITION SWITCH

Ignition switch failures are the most frequent so are wisely checked first. Find the wire from the ignition switch that leads to the ignition coil, disconnect it at the coil and turn on the ignition. Touch the detached wire momentarily to a ground. Watch for a faint spark. No spark indicates a failure in the switch or in wiring or connections between the battery and the coil. If the wire did spark when touched to a ground, reconnect it to the coil before proceeding.

CHECKING COIL CIRCUIT

Though the coil supplies electrical power to the distributor cap and from there to the spark plugs, it is energized and timed by the contact points inside the distributor. Therefore, checking the coil also requires testing the points.

First remove the distributor cap. Check it and the distributor rotor (on the shaft below the cap) for fractures and worn metal parts. Check the center carbon contact (button) in the distributor cap. The button should extend from the cap, be clean and have no cracks.

Turn the engine by hand slowly (grasping the fan belt and pulley) until the contact points are fully apart. After removing the high-tension coil lead from the distributor cap (center wire), turn on the ignition switch. With a small screwdriver, firmly short-circuit the movable contact point to the fixed contact point while holding the disconnected high-tension wire approximately ¼ inch from a ground. Repeated contact and breaking of the circuit with the screwdriver should give an intermittent spark from the high-tension wire to ground. A weak spark, or none at all, means there is a bad ignition coil or faulty wiring between the distributor points and the coil.

Inspection of Contact Points

While the contact points are still positioned fully apart, make checks to determine if they should be cleaned or replaced or if the condenser is bad.

First, inspect the points for pits and discoloration. Second, with the ignition switched on, firmly slide a screwdriver slowly down the side of the movable contact almost to the base of the distributor. As the screwdriver gets closer, electricity should arc to the base. If there is no spark or the spark is not strong and distinct, the problem is in the condenser or in the distributor wiring.

Next, have the engine cranked by the starter while closely observing the opening and closing of the contact points. An arc should occur between the points just as they begin to break contact. Again the spark must be strong and distinct. Poor arcing shows that the points should be cleaned or replaced. No arcing indicates that the wiring within the distributor is faulty or the condenser is bad.

If these two tests showed no sparking across the contact points, inspect the primary and ground wiring in the distributor and then test the condenser.

Primary Circuit Wiring Check

The coil primary wire that attaches (within the condenser) to the contact-point assembly terminal sometimes becomes twisted, frayed, or shorted (often intermittently) to the housing. Another problem could be a broken ground (pigtail) wire between the contact-point assembly plate and the distributor housing. Closely inspect the wiring for faults.

Condenser Check

Detach and isolate the condenser housing from the distributor while leaving the condenser lead on its terminal. Hand-turn the engine to open the points fully and then short-out the movable contact point by slowly sliding the screwdriver (against the contact) down toward the distributor base. If the spark occurs across the gap between the screwdriver and ground, the condenser has a short-circuit and must be replaced. To test out a condenser positively is difficult to do and perhaps not worth the time. It is best to replace a suspected condenser.

Fuel System Checks

Troubleshooting the fuel system for starting problems normally requires a check of the carburetors, fuel pump, tank and fuel lines for fuel restriction. A less common no-start problem is chronic carburetor flooding.

Checking Carburetors

In the previous section (*Locating No-Start Problems*), the throttle linkage was worked up and own by hand to check fuel ejection into the carb throats by the accelerator jets. No-start fuel problems most often involve the situation in which no gasoline reaches the carburetors.

In rare instances, *stale* gasoline will prevent starting. To test for stale fuel, prime the engine by squirting fresh gas into the carb throats. If the engine kicks over—analyze the gas in the tank by removing a small sample to a distant, safe area and cautiously attempt to ignite it.

If there is no fuel at the carburetors, check the tank, lines and fuel pump. First, look for an improperly vented cap. Remove gas cap and attempt to start engine. If it starts, cap is improperly vented. Just in case the gauge has failed, next check for gasoline in the tank, by shaking car and listening for sloshing sound.

Fuel Pump Test

If lacking gas at the carburetor, disconnect the fuel pump outlet line. WARNING: *to safeguard against dangerous sparks, first remove the high tension coil-distributor wire.* Cranking the engine should force fuel out of the line in steady spurts. A further test is to disconnect the input line of the fuel pump, hold a thumb on the input fitting while cranking the engine, and test for suction from the pump. No suction indicates that the fuel-pump diaphragm is leaking—maybe perforated—or that the diaphragm linkage is worn. Check the crankcase for gasoline. Often a ruptured diaphragm will leak fuel into the engine. A broken or worn cam shaft or cam lobe could also be the defect.

Checking Tank and Lines

Good suction at the pump input indicates a restricted fuel line to the tank or a clogged tank filter. Drain tank, blow compressed air through the line from the fuel pump, and then flush tank.

TEST FOR VAPOR LOCK

Fuel lines in areas exposed to excessive heat should be insulated because gasoline vaporizes when heated. The vapor bubbles prevent fuel flow to the carburetors and thus starve the engine for gas. If vapor forms and stalls the engine, let it cool if possible before trying to restart it.

Hard Starting, Poor Performance—Tuning

Many who have the "If it works, don't fool with it" attitude find that when they have car trouble, it is a major and expensive problem. A smarter approach that assures maximum car enjoyment is to keep an alert eye and ear on the car's daily performance. In addition, a semi-annual tune-up (Spring, Autumn) most economically maintains good performance.

A thorough tune-up should include a close inspection of the major mechanical parts and lubricating system of the engine as well as the normal electrical and fuel system overhaul. Ideal instruments for quickly checking mechanical engine parts are compression and vacuum gauges and a short piece of hose (a makeshift stethoscope).

These devices and other simple tools are used in the following step-by-step troubleshooting and tune-up procedures.

Spark Plugs and Wiring Check

After removing the spark plugs, carefully inspect them for cracked or broken porcelain and loose electrodes. Compare the condition of the spark plugs to that of the plugs illustrated to identify the cause of poor performance. In general, the symptoms are indicated by the color of the plugs: tan or medium gray—proper carburetion, plug in good working order; black—fuel mixture too rich, gap too wide, plug too cold; light gray—fuel mixture too lean, plug loose or leaking, valves not closing fully, plug too hot. Oily plugs might indicate that oil has been sucked into combustion chamber due to worn cylinders or piston rings or improper crank-

case venting. Also possible, if only one or two plugs are affected, is plug misfiring from poor or broken electrical circuit.

Spark plugs with minor carbon and oxide deposits can be cleaned, adjusted and reinstalled. Clean the plugs in a sandblasting machine or carefully by hand with a fine wire brush taking care not to scratch the porcelain. Dry carbon dust is best blown off with compressed air; oily plugs can be washed with a solvent.

Set the electrode gap by bending the outside electrode to the proper clearance. Never bend the center electrode. See specifications for spark plug types and recommended gaps.

Spark plugs should not be reset more than once because the point-of-heat changes as the center electrode wears back toward the insulator. Place a new compression gasket on each plug and tighten with only enough force to crush the gasket (normally ½ turn after seated by hand).

WIRING

Spark plug wiring should be removed, cleaned with a kerosene-moistened cloth, wiped dry and then carefully inspected for brittle, cracked, gummy or otherwise deteriorated insulation. Aged wiring permits electrical spark leakage . . . the cause of engine misses and crossfiring. Defective wiring should be replaced. Inspect and clean the wire terminals, spark plug terminals, and the distributor cap sockets to assure perfect electrical contact.

DISTRIBUTOR

After removing the distributor cap, inspect it for carbon paths which accumulate in areas of high voltage leakage. Discard the cap if any are present. Otherwise, clean the inside of the cap and check for cracks. Remove corrosion from the copper contacts and inspect the condition of the center (carbon) button. The button should extend from the cap, be clean and without cracks. If any contacts are deeply scored, replace the cap.

Inspect the distributor rotor for burns and, if necessary, replace it. With the rotor arm off, lubricate the distributor cam with non-corrosive high temperature grease. (NOTE: do not allow grease or dirt to contaminate breaker points.) De-

Carbon fouled   Oil fouled   Electrodes worn   Heavily coated

Overheated   Melted   Splash fouled   Bent electrode

Carbon Fouled Plugs
If only one plug is carbon fouled and others are normal, check ignition wiring for a break or loose connections. A compression check might indicate mechanical trouble in that cylinder.
If all plugs are sooted, fuel mixture might be too rich, spark gap could be too large, or the plug heat value is too high.

Oil Fouled Plugs
Plugs may have been "drowned" with fuel during cranking. If choke operates properly, fouling could be caused by poor oil control. A hotter plug is needed.

Excessive Electrode Gap
If all plugs have brown-gray deposits and electrode wear from .008″ to .010″ greater than original gap, they are completely worn. Replace entire set.

Heavily Coated Plugs
Heavy deposits, if easily flaked off, result from scavenger additives used in some brands of fuel. Though this accumulation creates heat buildup, its chemical nature causes only minimum electrical shorting. Replacement plugs should have same heat range.

Chipped Insulator
If one or two plugs in a set have chipped insulator tips, severe detonation was the likely cause. Bending the center electrode during gapping can also crack the insulator. Replace with new plugs of the correct gap and heat range. Check for over-advanced timing.

Normal, Usable Plugs
Plugs with evenly-colored light tan or gray deposits and moderate electrode wear (.005 gap growth) can be cleaned, regapped, and reinstalled.

All Plugs Overheated
If set has dead white insulators and badly eroded electrodes (.001″ erosion per 1,000 miles), check ignition timing for over-advance. Install next colder heat range.

One Plug Badly Burned
If one plug in a set has melted electrodes, preignition was likely encountered in that cylinder; check for intake manifold air leaks and possible cross fire. Be sure the one plug is not the wrong heat range.

Mechanical Damage
A broken insulator and bent electrodes result from some foreign object falling into the combustion chamber. If valves overlap, objects can travel from one cylinder to another. Always clean out cylinders to prevent recurrence.

One or Two Plugs "Splashed" Fouled
Some plugs in a relatively new set may have splashed deposits. This may occur after a long-delayed tune-up when accumulated cylinder deposits are thrown against the plugs at high engine rpm. Clean and reinstall these plugs.

Bent Side Electrodes
Improperly gapping plugs will weaken side electrode and alter electrical performance of spark plug.

Tune-Up Specifications

Engine Model	Spark Plugs Make, Type	Gap (in.)	Distributor Point Dwell (deg.)	Point Gap (in.)	Basic Ignition Timing* (deg.) @ r.p.m.	Cranking Compress. Press. (p.s.i.)	Intake① Clear. (in.)	Exhaust① Clear. (in.)	Intake④ Opens (deg.)	Idle Speed
B-14	Champion Y4A/J6	.028-.032	47	.018-.022	20 BTDC @ 1,500		.020	.020	0 @ TDC	
B-16A	Bosch W175T3	.028-.032	47-53	.016-.020	19-21 BTDC @ 1,500	135-150	.016	.018	10 BTDC	
B-16B	Bosch W225T3	.028-.032	47-53	.016-.020	21-23 BTDC @ 1,500	142-156	.020	.020	0 @ TDC	
B-18A	Bosch W175T1	.028-.032	59-65	.016-.020	21-23 BTDC @ 1,500	156-185	.016-.018	.016-.018	10 ATDC	500-700
B-18B	Bosch W225T1	.028-.032	59-65	.016-.020	17-19 BTDC @ 1,500 ③	170-200	.020-.022	.020-.022	0 @ TDC	600-800
B-18D	Bosch W175T1	.028-.032	59-65	.016-.020	22-24 BTDC @ 1,500 ②	156-185	.016-.018	.016-.018	10 ATDC	
B-20A	Bosch W175T35	.028-.032	59-65	.016-.020	21-23 BTDC @ 1,500	156-185	.016-.018	.016-.018	10 ATDC	700
B-20B	Bosch W200T35	.028-.032	59-65	.016-.020	10 BTDC @ 600-800	156-185	.020-.022	.020-.022	0 @ TDC	700
B-30A	Bosch W175T35	.028-.032	37-43	.010	10 BTDC @ 600-800	156-185	.020-.022	.020	0 @ TDC	750

NOTE: Emission control requires a precise approach to tune-up. Timing and idle speed are peculiar to the engine and its application, rather than to the engine alone. Data for the particular application will be found on a sticker in the engine compartment.

*With vacuum line disconnected.

① Either hot or cold.

② Some models with B-18D engines are set at 17-19° BTDC @ 1,500 rpm. Check the owner's manual and engine compartment sticker.

③ B-18B with emission controls — 5° BTDC @ 800 rpm.

④ When checking camshaft setting, adjust valves on cold engine to:

.045	B-16B
.043	B-16A, B-18A, B-18D, B-20A
.057	B-20B, B-30A.

tailed instructions for overhauling the distributor to specifications are given in Chapter 5.

Checking Points, Condenser, Connections

Carefully examine the contact (often called breaker) assemblies in the distributor for the following poor-performance conditions:

1. Points are blackened, pitted, or worn excessively. (Points in extended service normally become dull gray without losing efficiency).

2. Movable contact-point arm has lost spring action.

3. Fiber rubbing block on breaker is badly worn or loose.

4. Coil primary wire (attached to the breaker assembly with the condenser) is twisted, frayed or shorted on the distributor plate.

5. Condenser lead connection is loose or damaged.

6. Ground wire (pigtail) between the breaker assembly plate and the distributor housing is frayed or loose.

If any of the distributor components is faulty, replace it and then identify and repair the fault so that the new part can

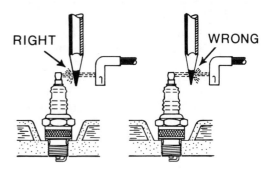

Coil polarity check.

give satisfactory service. Contact points that are slightly burned can be cleaned with a thin cut-stone or point file.

ADJUSTING POINT GAP

The breaker points must be correctly set before adjusting ignition timing. Turn the crankshaft until cam lobe on the distributor shaft has fully raised the breaker arm. Loosen the breaker plate hold-down screw and, using a feeler gauge, adjust the breaker gap to the correct setting by canting a screwdriver in the oval cutout. Then tighten the hold-down screw. Steps for adjusting distributor dwell angle with a dwell meter are listed in Chapter 5.

COIL AND POLARITY

An ignition coil having reversed polarity could reduce spark plug efficiency as much as 20%. The result would be a drastic loss of power.

Briefly inspect the coil housing for weak spots and cracks (especially around the tower) caused by high-voltage leaks or deterioration.

A check to determine if the ignition polarity matches the negative-to-ground (or positive-to-ground) circuitry of the battery can easily be made in any of three ways.

A. For negative-to-ground systems, firmly attach a "high-reading" voltmeter positive lead to engine ground (connect negative lead to ground for positive-to-ground system). Then, momentarily touch the other lead of the voltmeter to the secondary-circuit coil wire that leads to the distributor cap. A positive (up-scale) voltage reading indicates correct polarity. A negative (down-scale) reading shows a reversed polarity that will cause hard starting and premature wear of ignition components.

B. An optional test is to hold a soft-lead wood pencil in the gap between a disconnected spark plug cable and plug (or ground). With the engine cranking, observe the direction of spark jump between the wire and plug. "Flaring" of spark on the plug side of the pencil means that polarity is correct.

C. "Dishing" on the electrode side indicates wrong polarity. If polarity is wrong, reverse the two primary leads at the ignition coil.

SETTING IGNITION TIMING

If you have not set the breaker point gap, do so before proceeding. See paragraph, *Adjusting Point Gap*.

Next, turn the crankshaft until the Top Dead Center mark on the crankshaft pulley is in line with a raised spot on the timing gear cover. (The B14 and B16 engines have timing marks on the flywheel.) The No. 1 cylinder is in firing position and the distributor rotor should directly face the No. 1 cylinder spark-plug-wire contact in the distributor cap. (A notch in the housing of the distributor indicates that position.)

With TDC marks aligned, follow these steps:

1. Remove the rotor arm.
2. Loosen clamp screw at base of distributor body.
3. Connect a 12-volt test lamp in series between the distributor primary post and a ground.
4. Turn on the ignition.
5. Turn distributor body clockwise until the light goes out (contacts closed), then turn slowly counterclockwise until the exact moment the points open and the light goes on again.
6. Tighten distributor clamp screw.
7. Reinstall rotor arm and distributor cap.
8. Check ignition timing with a strobe light (if available) while engine is idling at 500 rpm and all vacuum hoses are disconnected from the distributor and plugged. Chapter 5 provides detailed steps for setting dwell angle and ignition timing.

Checking Vacuum

The vacuum gauge shows the difference in pressure between the inside and outside of the intake manifold. Since atmospheric pressure varies with altitude and changes daily with the weather, the action of the vacuum gauge needle is more indicative than any specific pressure valve. In general, the vacuum reading is less for higher elevation and also shows a drop from an extreme high-pressure weather system to a stormy, low pressure system. Pressure measurement is in inches. A well-tuned engine will give vacuum readings of between 18 and 20 inches at sea level.

READING A VACUUM

Attach the gauge to the intake manifold or on the engine side of the carburetor throttle butterfly. Warm the engine, set the idle speed between 800 and 1000 rpms, remove the air filter (in case it is partially clogged) and check to see that the carburetor chokes are open.

Make the first reading with the engine idling around 900 rpm. The needle should be steady and in the 18–20-inch range. If the pointer remains steady but at a substantially lower pressure, the poor performance problem affects power in all of the cylinders. It could be improper ignition or valve timing or an intake manifold leak. Improper valve timing normally gives the indicator a lower reading (7″-drop) than poor ignition timing (4″-drop). The size of a manifold leak determines where the indicator will stabilize. A severe warp or crack may reduce vacuum as much as 15 inches.

If the vacuum indicator wavers or fluctuates at idle rpm, the poor-performance problem normally affects only one or may-

	Vacuum Reading	Possible Reasons	Next Test
	Steady gauge reading 18–20″ at all speeds. Throttle is released and engine speed quickly cuts from over 2000 rpm to idle. Needle jumps 2–5″ above normal and then quickly drops to normal without pause or hesitation.	Normal engine performance.	Vacuum okay. Go to compression tests.
	Steady low reading. Figure A. (less than 2″ drop)	Retarded ignition timing.	Loosen clamp, rotate distributor to reset timing. Check gauge improvement.
	Steady, very low reading. Figure B.	Late valve timing.	Check valve timing. Make compression tests.
	Steady, extremely low reading. (up to 15″ drop) Figure C.	Severely warped or cracked intake manifold. Bad carburetor-to-manifold gasket.	Inspect manifold. Squirt oil around seal to detect leak.
	Pointer does not jump much above normal when throttle is quickly closed and engine speed is cut from above 2000 rpm to idle. Figure A.	Piston rings may be worn or defective and are blowing into crankcase.	Take compression test of cylinders to pinpoint trouble.
	Pointer jumps 2–5″ above normal upon quick deceleration but hesitates at higher pressure before returning to normal. Figure B.	Restricted exhaust system is causing backpressure on engine.	Check exhaust for dents, restrictions, clogged muffler.

	Vacuum Reading	*Possible Reasons*	*Next Test*
	Pointer (rhythmically drops 1–7″ below normal vacuum at regular intervals.	Leaking combustion chamber or valve; (ignition or plug failure involving one cylinder).	Make compression tests; (make ignition check).
	Pointer drops rapidly but intermittently (not every time) and then recovers.	Valve sticking at times won't close tight.	Note which valve sticks. Apply penetrating oil to one valve guide at a time. Problem will correct itself temporarily.
	Pointer wavers rapidly between 10–20″ at idle becoming worse with higher rpm.	Weak or broken spring causing valve to close slowly.	Remove valve covers; check condition of springs.
	Wavers irregularly at idle; fluctuates rapidly in smaller range at higher rpm.	Manifold leak at intake port—upsets and reduces cylinder draft.	Squirt oil around manifold; check vacuum increase when oil fills leak. Replace faulty gasket.
	Drifts at idle; stabilizes at higher engine rpm.	Burnt valve; combustion chamber leak.	Make compression tests.
	Wavers irregularly in one range despite engine speed.	Unbalanced carburetion; improper spark plug gap, ignition timing; poor valve seating.	Adjust carburetors; check plug gap; check distributor and advance spark; make compression tests.
	Vacuum averages lower than normal at idle, needle fluctuates almost 3″ on both sides of normal.	Worn valve guides admitting air—upsetting carburetion.	Squirt oil on guide seals. Check vacuum improvement.

be a few cylinders. Use the illustrated guide to interpret vacuum gauge readings.

Checking Compression

A second important instrument is the compression gauge used to measure pressure differences among cylinders. Pressure variations cause loss of power and poor idling.

Warm the engine to hot operating temperature, remove all spark plugs, prop open the throttle linkage so air is not restricted and affix the compression gauge to the spark plug opening.

Crank engine with throttle open and note gauge pointer reading after fifth revolution. Repeat procedure on each cylinder. All cylinders should be within ten pounds of each other and maintain an average pressure of around 150 psi. (See "Tune-up Specifications")

One or two low readings in the cylinders indicate trouble with valves, rings, pistons, or combustion-chamber leaks. Low compression readings in all cylinders indicate incorrect valve timing.

To determine the fault, squirt an ounce (approx.) of light oil into the low-compression cylinder, replace the compression gauge, and crank the engine another five revolutions for the second reading. If compression increases substantially, the rings are worn or stuck and need replacing.

No increase in compression after adding oil to the cylinder narrows the trouble to improper valve seating, a cracked or broken piston, or a combustion-chamber leak between the head and the cylinder.

First, check out the possibility of a combustion-chamber leak. Turn the engine while checking for hissing noises and perhaps a discharge of oil from the flange between the cylinder and the head. This indicates a poor seal between the cylinder head and the cylinder. A leaky head gasket can often be detected by loss of compression in two adjacent cylinders.

Detecting piston damage involves replacing all the spark plugs, starting the engine, and listening for a distinctive clicking noise at idle and upon acceleration. Combustion gasses (blow-by) will also escape into the crankcase through the piston crack. See TROUBLESHOOTING ENGINE NOISES, in this chapter.

Abnormal Oil Consumption

Another way to identify poor-performance troubles is a check of oil consumption. Continual addition of oil, fouled spark plugs and blue-gray exhaust smoke are obvious signs.

Worn or broken piston rings permit oil to enter the combustion-chamber and reduce burning efficiency. In addition, poor rings permit combustion gases to enter the crankcase. This hot "blow-by" changes the crankcase oil into vapor that escapes through the ventilating system. Blow-by also pressurizes the crankcase, forcing oil leakage through the weak pan seals.

Worn valve guides fail to keep oil out of the combustion-chamber, resulting in poor performance and excessive oil consumption. Piston ring and valve guide replacement steps are detailed in Chapter 3.

Before assuming that engine wear is the cause of excessive oil usage, make a thorough inspection for external leaks. After placing clean paper underneath the engine, run the engine at medium speed until the oil is hot. Stop the engine and check for oil drippings on the paper. Trace the leak to its source and correct it. In many cases the leak is the sole cause of abnormal oil consumption. It's been estimated that a single drop of oil lost every fifty feet will amount to a full quart every 500 miles, an amount worth saving.

Greater oil consumption is normal if the oil used is too light or if the engine is run often at high speeds. A break-in period for new rings also requires additional oil.

High Ring Friction

In a newly rebuilt engine, poor performance is sometimes due to too much ring friction. Firm expander springs often press the rings too tightly against the cylinder walls. Engine power and gas economy drop conspicuously.

Test for excessive ring friction by holding the throttle open to an engine speed of 1000 rpm. Then turn off the ignition. An engine with proper tension will slow to stop and then roll back and forth momentarily. An engine with tight rings will stop suddenly without rolling.

Adjusting Valve Clearance

Improper valve clearance adjustment

results in loss of power and possible valve damage. Excessive clearance can be detected by noisy valves. Insufficient clearance causes valves to burn and possible backfiring through the carburetor.

When the engine is at operating temperature, remove the air cleaner and rocker cover. Turn the engine over by hand until the pushrod stops falling—the valve is fully closed at this point.

Basic valve-clearance adjustment for each cylinder is at the point where both valves are closed, TDC of the piston's compression stroke. Follow the firing order of the engine which is 1-3-4-2. Final adjustment of all valves is when the engine is at operating temperature and slowly idling. See Chapter 3 for details of valve adjustment.

Troubleshooting Engine Noises

If engine noises can be located and analyzed before the engine is disassembled, correcting the problem is much easier. Of course fine tuning is not possible until mechanical engine troubles are repaired. For locating noises, a piece of water hose of convenient length is a handy substitute for a stethoscope.

Valve Noises

Valve noise is a loud rhythmic clicking that varies directly with rpm, but occurs at half the beat of other engine noises because the camshaft rotates at half the engine speed.

Remove the valve covers to help locate noises better. Set engine rpm to the speed where the noise is most pronounced. If needed, hold end of piece of hose half an inch from tappets and listen to one valve at a time until the noisemaker is identified.

Sticky valves and tappets with excessive clearance have similar sounds although sticking-valve noises are normally intermittent. Check for excessive tappet clearance by inserting a feeler gauge between the noisy valve stem and its tappet. If the noise stops, reset the clearance. Remember, valves will burn if clearance is reduced below factory specifications. Valve sticking becomes pronounced when the engine idles after having been run hard. As the idling engine cools to its normal operating temperature the stick-

ing-valve noise lessens. When a valve sticks, the lost compression from improper closing makes the engine idle roughly.

Warped and burnt valves also cause the engine to run irregularly, especially under low-speed load. They sometimes click but more often make hissing, wheezing sounds through the exhaust manifold (exhaust valve) or back fire (intake valve) through the carburetor.

Broken springs and bent valve stems don't close valves properly and are noisy as well.

Loose rocker arms and bent or worn pushrods transmit heavy rattling sounds.

Piston Noises

Generally, piston noises result from a piston slapping from side to side in its bore due to excessive clearance. However, if the piston noise is faint in a cold engine and disappears shortly after the engine reaches operating temperature, the condition might not be worth special attention.

Individual piston noises can be detected by shorting out one spark plug at a time while the engine is under partial load until the noise ceases. The piston makes no noise when its spark plug doesn't fire. A collapsed or badly worn piston makes a lowpitched, dull, metallic noise when the engine is under a load.

Broken rings or a cylinder ridge not removed when installing new rings will produce a steady, clicking, metallic noise at all engine speeds.

Loose wrist pins give a sharp metallic knock that is more noticeable when the engine is idling. Speeding up the engine to about 1500 rpm and then releasing the throttle is another way to detect the wrist pin knock.

Crankshaft Bearing Noises

Crankshaft noises can be grouped into main bearing noise, connecting rod noise, and crankshaft end-play noise.

A loose main bearing gives a heavy bumping noise when the engine is under load.

A loose connecting rod bearing has a steady rap after letting up slightly on the accelerator when car is driven about 50 mph. Shorting one spark plug at a time relieves pressure on each connecting rod bearing in turn and thereby deadens the noise of the defective bearing.

Excessive crankshaft end-play can be heard as a thud each time the clutch pedal is depressed. A rasping noise, when speeding and slowing the engine, indicates a loose fly wheel.

DETONATION

Detonation, an explosion rather than a smooth burning of the fuel in a cylinder, is caused by an imbalance of compression, heat, fuel, valves, and timing. Detonation can be devastating to engine parts. Each of the following problems must be eliminated to prevent detonation.

A. Excessive cooling system temperature
B. Insufficient spark plug heat range
C. Over-advanced ignition timing
D. Too-low fuel octane rating
E. Lean carburetor fuel mixture
F. Stuck manifold heat control valve

With the ignition system checked, the vacuum and compression readings interpreted, and engine noises investigated, the mechanic should have a good indication of any mechanical defects in the engine. These malfunctions should be corrected before attempting to tune the engine. Detailed overhaul procedures for the ignition system and engine mechanical parts are provided in later chapters.

Cleaning Fuel System

A final pre-tune-up step involves cleaning the carburetors, fuel filters and, if necessary, lines and tank.

Many fuel system problems result from accumulation of water, dirt, and gummy residues in the tank, lines. and pump. Other problems are caused by restricted tank ventilation, leaky lines and connections, and worn out moving parts. These troubles, when identified before disassembly, can be eliminated efficiently.

Ideally, the carburetor should be taken apart, cleaned thoroughly, and reassembled with new gasketing and other non-metal parts. If complete disassembly is not feasible, it is recommended that carburetor jets be removed from time to time and blown through with compressed air. Wash carburetor housing with gasoline (engine COLD) to remove dirt. Remove only one jet at a time for cleaning to prevent a mistake on replacement.

(NOTE: the jets should not be cleaned with a sharp or abrasive object that might cause deformation of the close factory calibration.)

CHECKING FUEL-AIR MIXTURES

Poor engine performance can be caused by air-fuel mixtures that are either too rich or too lean. Both maladjustments are harmful to the engine. A lean mixture at high speeds overheats the combustion chambers to the point where valves might burn. A rich mixture washes lubricating oil from the cylinders, resulting in scuffed rings and scored cylinder walls.

Rub paper or cloth around the inside of the exhaust pipe, checking for carbon deposits. A rich mixture leaves a black residue.

Choke off the carburetor(s) while the warmed engine is running at 1500 rpm. (The palm of the hand can be used to restrict incoming air.) By reducing the air flow, the air-fuel mixture is normally enriched and the engine speeds up somewhat. If it doesn't speed up at all, the mixture adjustment is *too rich;* if it speeds up drastically, the mixture adjustment is *too lean.*

When a carburetor has a lean mixture, the engine pauses and then accelerates poorly with apparent sponginess (there might be backfiring). If a weak fuel pump or restricted gas line is the cause of the lean mixture, the engine runs out of fuel at higher engine speeds.

Rich mixture can be caused by high fuel pressure forcing the needle valve from its seat. The carburetor floods and performance breaks down.

A malfunctioning carburetor cannot be tuned, so should be overhauled. Detailed procedures are in Chapter 3.

CLEANING FUEL FILTERS

Loosen the cover hex bolt and remove the screen from the mechanical fuel pump. Wash screen and cover in solvent and blow dry with air. Replace gasket if necessary and reinstall screen, cover and bolt. Then start engine and check for leaks.

CLEANING AIR FILTERS

To clean the dry paper filter, remove and tap lightly to loosen dirt, or blow out with compressed air. Restricted filters will adversely affect engine performance. If too dirty, replace the element.

Oil-wetted, metal-mesh filters can be washed in solvent. Blow out with compressed air or let dry in the open. Re-oil lightly prior to installation.

Cleaning Carburetor Parts

All carburetors have numerous small passages that can be fouled by carbon and gummy deposits. Metal parts should

Piston damaged by inaudible detonation and pre-ignition at high speeds.

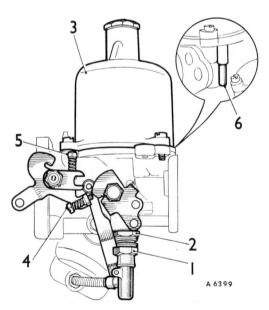

A 6399

The Type HS Carburetor

1. Jet adjusting nut
2. Jet locking nut
3. Piston/suction chamber
4. Fast-idle adjusting screw
5. Throttle adjusting screw
6. Piston lifting pin

Tuning
Single Carburetors

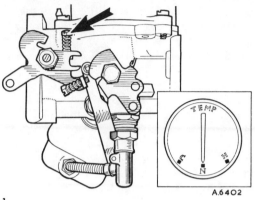

A.6402

1.
A. Warm engine up to normal temperature.
B. Switch off engine.
C. Unscrew the throttle adjusting screw until it is just clear of its stop and the throttle is closed.
D. Set throttle adjusting screw 1½ turns open.

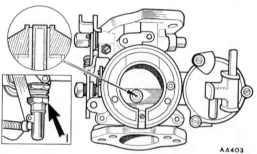

A.6403

2.
A. Mark for reassembly and remove piston/suction chamber unit.
B. Disconnect mixture control wire.
C. Screw the jet adjusting nut (1) until the jet is flush with the bridge of the carburetor or fully up if this position cannot be obtained.

A6335A

3.
A. Replace the piston/suction chamber unit as marked.
B. Check that the piston falls freely onto the bridge when the lifting pin (6) is released. If not, see items 15, 16 and 17.
C. Turn down the jet adjusting nut (1) two complete turns.

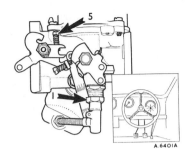

A.6401A

4.

A. Restart the engine and adjust the throttle adjusting screw (5) to give desired idling as indicated by the glow of the ignition warning light.

B. Turn the jet adjusting nut (1) up to weaken or down to richen until the fastest idling speed consistent with even running is obtained.

C. Readjust the throttle adjusting screw (5) to give correct idling if necessary.

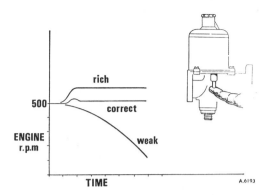

A.6193

6.

A. Check for correct mixture by gently pushing the lifting pin up about $\frac{1}{32}$ in. (.8 mm.) after free movement has been taken up.

B. The graph illustrates the effect on engine rpm when the lifting pin raises the piston, indicating the mixture strength.
Rich mixture: rpm increases considerably.
Correct mixture: rpm increases very slightly.
Weak mixture: rpm immediately decreases.

C. Readjust the mixture strength if necessary.

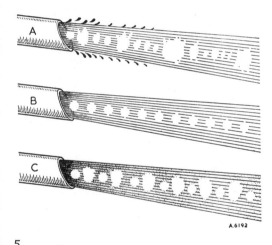

A.6192

5.

The effect of mixture strength on exhaust smoke.

A. Too weak: irregular note, splashy misfire and colorless.

B. Correct: regular and even note.

C. Too rich: regular or rhythmical, blackish.

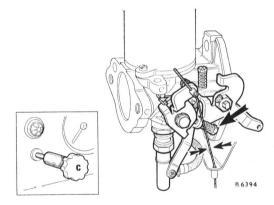

B.6394

7.

A. Reconnect the mixture control wire with about $\frac{1}{16}$ in. (1.6 mm.) free movement before it starts to pull on the jet lever.

B. Pull the mixture control knob until the linkage is about to move the carburetor jet and adjust the fast-idle screw to give an engine speed of about 1,000 rpm when hot.

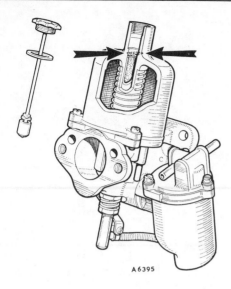

A 6395

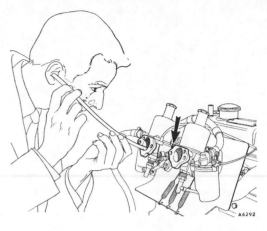

A6292

8.

Finally top up the piston damper with the recommended engine oil until the level is ½ in. (13 mm.) above the top of the hollow piston rod.

Note: On dust-proofed carburetors, identified by a transverse hole drilled in the neck of the suction chambers and no vent hole in the damper cap, the oil level should be ½ in. (13 mm.) below the top of the hollow piston rod.

Tuning
Multi-Carburetors

Remove the air cleaners and carry out item 1 as for single on all carburetors; then:

10.

A. Restart the engine and adjust the throttle adjusting screws on each carburetor to give the desired idling speed as indicated by the glow of the ignition warning light.

B. Compare the intensity of the intake "hiss" on all carburetors and alter the throttle adjusting screws until the "hiss" is the same.

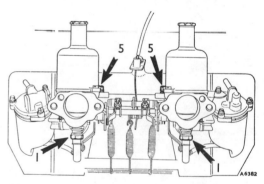

A6382

11.

A. Turn the jet adjusting nuts (1) on all carburetors up to weaken or down to richen by the same amount until the fastest idling speed consistent with even running is obtained.

B. Readjust the throttle adjusting screws (5) to give correct idling if necessary.

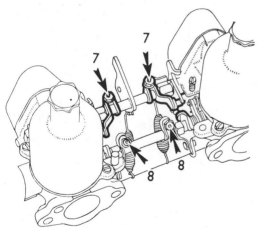

9.

A. Slacken both of the clamping bolts (7) on the throttle spindle interconnections.

B. Disconnect the jet control interconnection by slackening the clamping bolts (8).

C. Carry out items 2 and 3 as for single carburetors, then additionally:

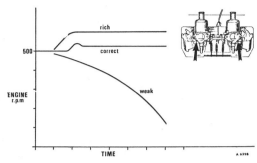

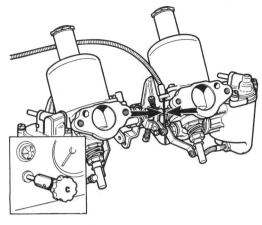

12.

A. Check for correct mixture by gently pushing the lifting pin of the front carburetor up $\frac{1}{32}$ in. (. 8mm.) after free movement has been taken up. The graph illustrates the possible effect on engine rpm. Readjust the mixture strength if necessary.

B. Repeat the operation on the other carburetors and after adjustment recheck since they are all interdependent.

C. Item 5 shows the correct type of exhaust smoke.

14.

A. Reconnect the mixture control wire with about $\frac{1}{16}$ in. (1.6 mm.) free movement before it starts to pull on the jet levers.

B. Pull the mixture control knob until the linkage is about to move the carburetor jets, and adjust the fast idle screws, comparing the intensity of the air intake "hiss" to give an an engine speed of about 1,000 rpm when hot.

C. Refit the air cleaners.

Adjusting and Servicing
Jet Centering

15.

The piston should fall freely onto the carburetor bridge with a click when the lifting pin is released with the jet in the fully up position. If it will do this only with the jet lowered, then the jet unit requires re-centering. This is done as follows:

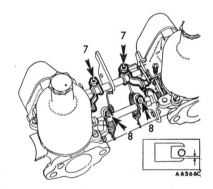

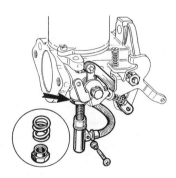

13.

A. Set the throttle interconnection clamping levers (7) so that the link pin is .006 in. (.15 mm.) away from the lower edge of the fork (see inset). Tighten the clamp bolts.

B. With both jet levers at their lowest position, set the jet interconnection lever clamp bolts (8) so that both jets begin to move simultaneously.

16.

A. Remove the jet head screw to release the control linkage.

B. Withdraw the jet, disconnecting the fuel feed pipe union in the float-chamber, and removing the rubber sealing washer. Remove the jet locking spring and adjusting nut.

C. Replace the jet and insert the fuel feed pipe connection into the float-chamber.

D. Slacken the jet locking nut until the assembly is free to rotate.

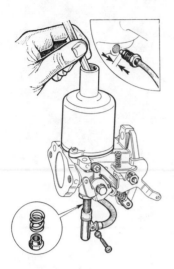

Float-Chamber Fuel Level

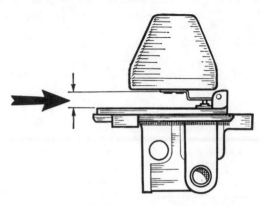

19.

A. Remove and invert the float-chamber lid.
B. With the needle valve held in the shut-off position by the weight of the float only, there should be a ⅛ to 3/16 in. (3.2 to 4.8 mm.) gap between the float lever and the rim of the float-chamber lid.
C. The float may be set by bending at the crank.

17.

A. Remove the piston damper and apply pressure to the top of the piston rod with a pencil.
B. Tighten the jet locking nut keeping the jet hard up against the jet bearing.
C. Finally check again as in item 15.
D. Re-fit the jet locking spring and adjusting nut. Before replacing the fuel feed pipe in the float-chamber, fit the rubber sealing washer over the end of the plastic pipe so that at least 3/16 in. (4.8 mm.) of pipe protrudes (see inset). Reassemble the controls.
E. Refill the piston dampers with the recommended engine oil (see item 8).

Needle Size and Position

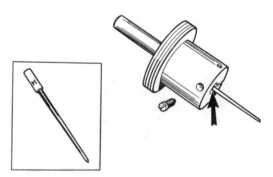

20.

A. The needle size is determined during engine development and will provide the correct mixture strength unless extremes of temperature, humidity, or altitude are encountered. At altitudes exceeding 6,000 ft. (1830 m.) a weaker needle will be necessary. A different needle may also be necessary if any alteration to the standard specification of the exhaust system, air cleaner, camshaft, or compression ratio is made.
B. To check that the correct needle is fitted: mark for reassembly and remove the piston/suction chamber unit.
C. Slacken the needle clamping screw, extract the needle, and check its identifying mark against the recommendation.
D. Replace the correct needle and lock it in position so that the shoulder on the shank is flush with the piston base.
E. Reassemble the piston/suction chamber unit as marked.

Cleaning

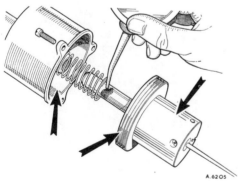

A.6205

18.

A. At the recommended intervals, mark for reassembly and carefully remove the piston/suction chamber unit.
B. Using an oil-moistened cloth, clean the inside bore of the suction chamber and the two diameters of the piston.
C. Lightly oil the piston rod only and reassemble as marked.
D. Refill piston damper (see item 8).

Summary

Symptom	Cause	Remedy	Item No.
Erratic running Stalling at idling	Sticking piston: Dirty piston and suction chamber	Clean	18
Lack of power High fuel consumption	Jet out of centre Bent needle	Re-centre Fit new	15, 16, and 17 20
Hesitation at pick-up	Low damper oil level Incorrect oil grade (too thin)	Top up Replace with correct grade	8 8
Fuel leak from float-chamber/feed pipe union	Rubber sealing washer displaced or damaged	Renew	17
Float-chamber flooding	Dirty or worn float-chamber needle valve (dirty fuel)	Clean or renew valve (flush system)	
	Punctured float Incorrect fuel level	Fit new Check and reset level	19

be soaked in carburetor solvent until thoroughly clean. However, the solvent will weaken or destroy cork, plastic and leather components. These parts should be wiped with a clean, lint-free cloth.

While the carburetor is disassembled, check the bowl cover with a straight edge for warped surfaces.

The needle valves and seats should be closely inspected for wear and damage. Replace these parts when imperfect because their performance affects engine tuning most critically.

After cleaning the parts, blow air through the high and low speed jets to ensure that all passages are clear.

Reassemble the carburetor, using new gaskets and other non-metal parts.

LUBRICATING CARBURETOR LINKAGE

Lubricate all pivot points with 1–2 drops of engine oil while moving throttle controls. Lubricate accelerator pump rods. Disconnect all ball joints, fill cups with grease, reconnect. Move linkage back and forth to check for proper functioning.

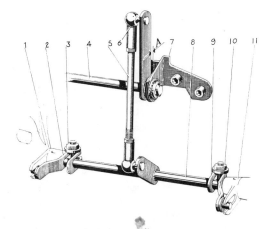

1. Lever on throttle spindle
2. Lever on intermediate spindle
3. Locknut
4. Control shaft
5. Link rod
6. Lock wire
7. Bracket
8. Intermediate shaft
9. Lever on intermediate shaft
10. Locknut
11. Lever on throttle spindle

Throttle rod linkage—B20B engine with SU-HS6 carburetors.

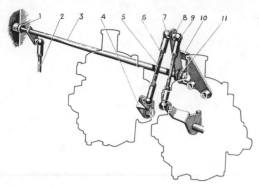

1. Bushing
2. Link rod for pedal
3. Control shaft
4. Lever
5. Link rod
6. Locknut
7. Ball joint
8. Lever
9. Lock wire
10. Bracket
11. Rubber mounting

Throttle rod linkage—B20B engine with Zenith-Stromberg 175 CD-2SE carburetors.

Adjusting the Carburetor

Of utmost importance in tuning is the reminder that carburetors can only be adjusted satisfactorily when the engine is in good condition and the timing is perfect. (Before adjusting fuel mixture on the carburetor, check the accelerator pump discharge at pump nozzles.)

Synchronizing Twin Carburetors

First warm up the engine, remove air cleaner, disconnect throttle linkage, and adjust for equal idling on the carburetors at a higher idling speed of 1000 to 1200 rpm.

If a carburetor synchronizing gauge is available, adjust it on one carburetor throat to a piston height near the middle of the scale. Switch the test gauge to the other carburetor and, if necessary, reset the air-adjustment screw of that carb until the synchronizing gauge piston returns to the middle position. NOTE: *do not reset the gauge level*

1968 and later cars have an intake manifold which heats the intake mixture by circulating it through baffles heated by the exhaust gases in the exhaust manifold. In addition to heating the mixture, the manifold also acts as a plenum chamber, and reduces the necessity of close synchronization of the carburetors.

Idle Adjustment—Zenith Stromberg 175-CD-2S/2SE

The 175-CD-2S/2SE carburetor contains a single jet with a tapered needle that is operated by an air valve and carburetor vacuum. There is no special idling system. The fuel air mixture is set at idling speed by the single adjusting screw at the bottom of the carburetor and applies to the entire speed range. There is no choke as such. Rather, a disc-like cold starting device, when actuated, depresses the jet, giving a richer mixture. Therefore, there are two adjustments, one for the proper fuel-air mixture and the fast idle stop screw for proper idling speed. To make these adjustments, remove the air cleaner and proceed as follows:

1. Press the air valve down, and screw in the fuel-air mixture adjusting screw at the bottom of the carburetor until the jet just touches the valve. Then unscrew the adjusting screw 1½ turns.

2. Run the engine until it is warm.

3. Adjust the fast idle stop screw for an idle speed of about 600 rpm.

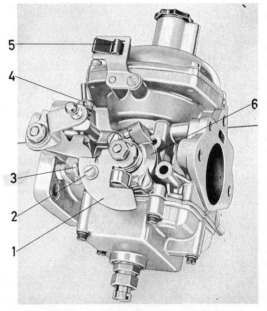

1. Choke cam
2. Choke control connection
3. Fast-idle stop screw
4. Throttle stop screw
5. Attaching sleeve for choke control
6. Cold start device

Zenith-Stromberg 175-CD-2S horizontal carburetor

4. Screw in the fuel mixture adjusting screw until the engine starts to run unevenly. Then slowly turn the screw in the opposite direction until the engine again starts to run unevenly. Finally turn the screw back to a point somewhere between these two positions.

5. Adjust the fast idle stop screw until it barely touches the choke cam at a point about one-half inch from the upper part of the cam when it is turned upwards. (In extremely cold weather, adjust the screw so that it touches the choke cam when the choke control is pushed in fully).

IDLE ADJUSTMENT—ZENITH 36VN

The down-draft Zenith 36VN has a hand regulated choke, fixed main and idling jets and an acceleration pump. Fuel air mixture at idling speed is controlled by an adjustment screw.

Adjust the carburetor for engine idling by first warming up the engine. At idling speed, screw in the fuel-air mixture idling adjustment until the engine speeds up. Then slowly unscrew the adjustment until the engine speeds up. Then slowly unscrew the adjustment until the engine idles slowly but evenly. Finally, screw in the adjustment until the engine just runs smoothly.

IDLE AND CHOKE ADJUSTMENT—SU-HS6

When starting with a cold engine the fuel-air mixture is enriched by a lowering of the jets through manual operation of the choke on the instrument panel. In addition, the fast idling screw is moved somewhat by a cam on the choke lever, opening the throttle plate slightly.

Obtain the proper fuel-air mixture and idling adjustment as follows after warming engine:

1. Adjust both carburetors at the same time. First, screw in the fuel-air mixture adjusting nut at the bottom of each carburetor to its upper position, and then back it off 1½ turns.

2. Adjust the idle screw on each carb equally and to obtain an engine idling speed of about 600 rpm. Turn the screws so that the intake sounds of the carbs are equal strength.

3. Without touching the idle screw, adjust the fuel-air mixture nut at the bottom of each carb one at a time, by first turning slowly downwards (richer mixture) and then upwards (leaner mixture) until the engine runs smoothly. The best position is reached when the highest engine speed is obtained without altering the idle adjusting screw.

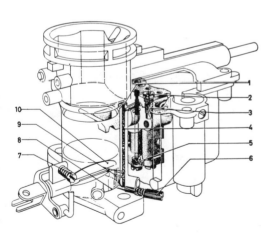

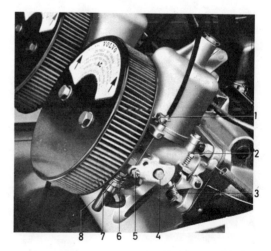

1. Air hole	6. Fuel-air mixture idling adjustment
2. Idling air jet	7. Fast-idle stop screw
3. Idling jet	8. Venturi
4. Idling channel	9. Transition holes
5. Main jet	10. Throttle flap

1. Attachment for choke control outer casing	5. Choke control locking screw
2. Idle adjusting screw	6. Locknut
3. Fast idle adjusting screw	7. Fuel-air mixture adjusting nut
4. Lever	8. Jet

Zenith 36VN down-draught carburetor.

Type S.U. carburetor.

4. Adjusting equally on both carburetors, adjust the idle screws for proper idling speed.

5. Check that the fuel-air mixture is correct, first in one carburetor then in the other by lifting the piston, using the pin beside the air intake.

The engine should run with about the same unevenness in both cases, and the speed should fall off to about 450 or 500 rpm. If the engine stalls when one of the carb pistons is lifted, the mixture in the other carb is too lean. If engine speed increases, the mixture in the other carb is too rich.

The choke control and fast idling adjustments are made as follows, keeping in mind that adjustments must always be made so that both carburetors are affected to exactly the same extent by the control:

1. Pull out choke control on the instrument panel about ⅝".

2. Loosen the locking screw for the choke control cable. Lift the lever enough to let the jet start to go down.

3. Adjust the fast idle screw so that it just touches the fast idle cam on the lever when the jet starts to go down as described in Step 3. Tighten the control cable locking screw.

4. Check that both carburetors are operated to the same extent by pulling the choke control cable and watching the jets go down. Adjust setting if jets do not go down equally.

Idle and Choke Adjustment (B14A and B16B Engines)

B14A engines employ twin horizontal Type SU-H2 carburetors, while B16B enines are equipped with twin horizontal SU-H4 types. Except for slight variations in float and choking arrangements, these carburetors are similar to the SU-HS6 twin carburetors and adjustment can be carried out as previously described for the B18B/D engines.

Exhaust Emission Control

Volvo has reduced the engine emissions by designing the engines to run very effi-

1. Hydraulic chamber
2. Suction chamber
3. Designation plate
4. Fuel line connection
5. Hose connection to air cleaner (float chamber vent)
6. Float chamber
7. Fuel line from float chamber to jet
8. Lever
9. By-pass valve
10. Primary throttle
11. Connection flange

SU-HS6 Carburetor, left side.

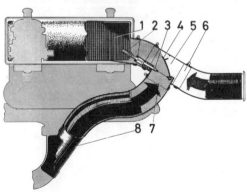

1. Air cleaner
2. Thermostat
3. Flap control
4. Flap
5. Flap housing
6. Cold air intake
7. Warm air intake
8. Heater plate on exhaust manifold

Emission control air preheater system.

gines run only if air, fuel, compression and spark are brought together in the cylinders at the same instant. This illustration shows a typical electrical system, the nerve center of any engine, with its major parts interconnected. The system includes the starting circuit (battery, solenoid and starter), the spark circuit (coil, condenser, breaker points, rotor and spark plugs), and the charging circuit (generator and regulator-cutout). Keeping the electrical system in good order eliminates most sources of engine trouble.

THE ELECTRI

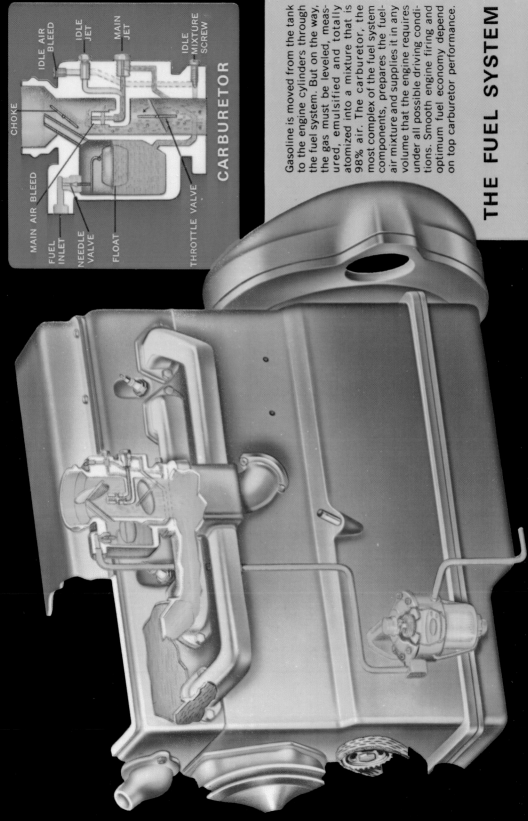

THE FUEL SYSTEM

CARBURETOR

CHOKE

IDLE AIR BLEED

IDLE JET

MAIN JET

IDLE MIXTURE SCREW

MAIN AIR BLEED

FUEL INLET

NEEDLE VALVE

FLOAT

THROTTLE VALVE

Gasoline is moved from the tank to the engine cylinders through the fuel system. But on the way, the gas must be leveled, measured, emulsified and totally atomized into a mixture that is 98% air. The carburetor, the most complex of the fuel system components, prepares the fuel-air mixture and supplies it in any volume that the engine requires under all possible driving conditions. Smooth engine firing and optimum fuel economy depend on top carburetor performance.

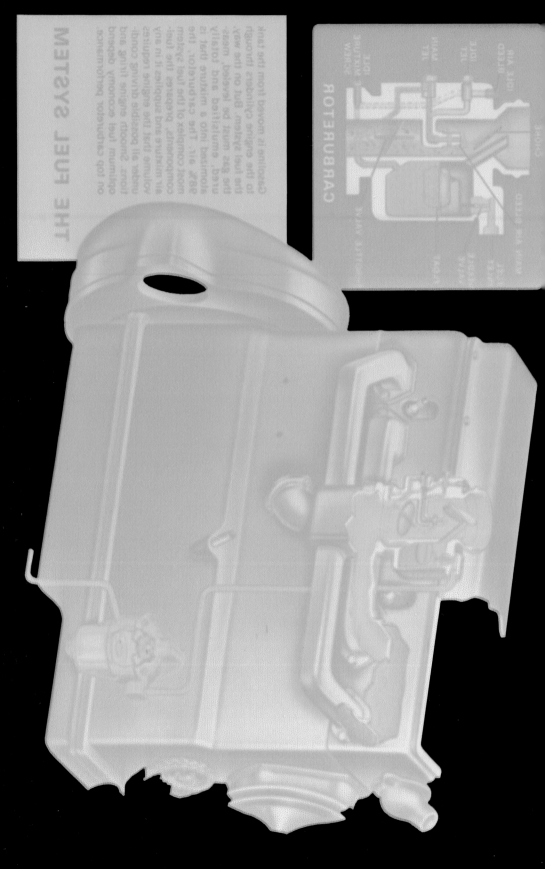

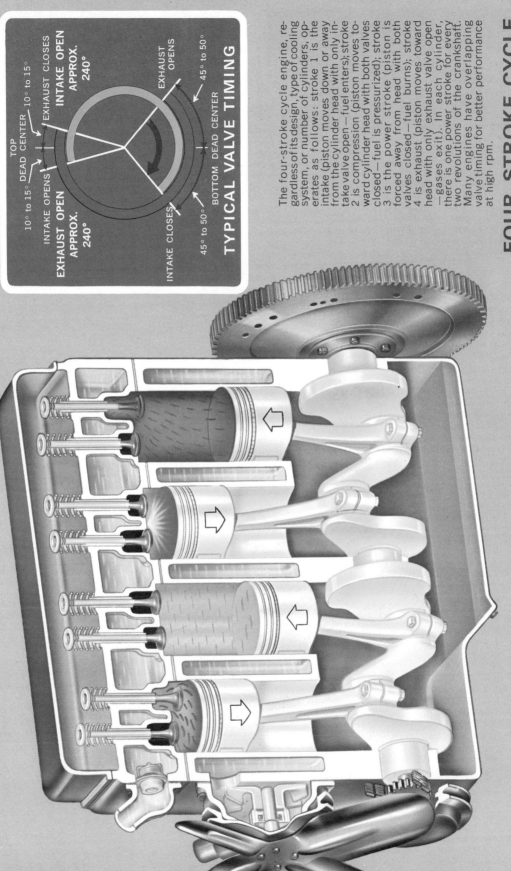

TYPICAL VALVE TIMING

TOP
DEAD CENTER 10° to 15°

10° to 15°

INTAKE OPENS

EXHAUST CLOSES

EXHAUST OPEN
APPROX.
240°

INTAKE OPEN
APPROX.
240°

EXHAUST OPENS

45° to 50°

INTAKE CLOSES

45° to 50°

BOTTOM DEAD CENTER

FOUR-STROKE CYCLE

The four-stroke cycle engine, regardless of its design, type of cooling system, or number of cylinders, operates as follows: stroke 1 is the intake (piston moves down or away from the cylinder head with only intake valve open—fuel enters); stroke 2 is compression (piston moves toward cylinder head with both valves closed—fuel is pressurized); stroke 3 is the power stroke (piston is forced away from head with both valves closed—fuel burns); stroke 4 is exhaust (piston moves toward head with only exhaust valve open—gases exit). In each cylinder, there is one power stroke for every two revolutions of the crankshaft. Many engines have overlapping valve timing for better performance at high rpm.

ciently. Carburetor intake air is kept at a constant temperature by a thermostatic valve which mixes cold outside air and warm air heated by the exhaust manifold. This allows the carburetors to be set at a very efficient mixture, and to always hold the mixture, regardless of outside air temperature.

The fuel-air mixture is heated in the intake manifold in a preheating chamber. The exhaust manifold heats baffles in the intake manifold which heats the fuel-air mixture as it passes around the baffles.

By keeping temperatures of the air and fuel-air mixture constant, the engine can be tuned to run very efficiently, without any compensation for changes in air temperature.

The distributor is equipped with a vacuum advance unit, which gives a greater range of ignition timing than before. At idle and during deceleration, the timing is retarded considerably to reduce the quantity of unburned gases, but advances normally during acceleration and high speed running.

Clutch Troubleshooting

Clutch slippage, chatter, and grabbing are most noticeable when accelerating from a standstill in first or reverse gears.

Dragging of the clutch is obvious when shifting between gears, especially into and out of reverse.

DRAGGING—fails to release completely
  a. Excessive linkage free play
  b. Sticking or faulty pilot bearing
  c. Damaged clutch plates (pressure and/or driven)
  d. Release yoke off pivot ball-stud
  e. Driven-plate hub binding on main drive gear spline

SLIPPING—does not firmly engage
  a. Insufficient linkage free play
  b. Oil-soaked driven disc (correct oil leak before installing new assembly)
  c. Worn or damaged driven disc
  d. Warped pressure plate or flywheel
  e. Weak diaphragm spring (replace cover assembly)
  f. Driven plate not seated (make 20–50 normal starts)
  g. Driven plate overheated (check lash after cooled)

GRABBING-CHATTER—intermittent seizing and slipping
  a. Oil spotted, burned or glazed facings
  b. Worn splines on main drive gear or clutch disc
  c. Loose engine or drive train mountings
  d. Warped pressure plate, clutch disc or flywheel
  e. Burned or smeared resin on flywheel or pressure plate (sand

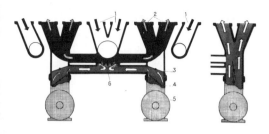

1. Exhaust manifold
2. Intake manifold
3. Secondary throttle
4. Primary throttle
5. Carburetor
6. Preheating Chamber

Emission control manifold heating system—B20B engine.

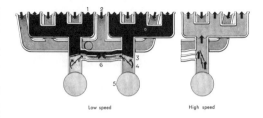

1. Intake manifold
2. Exhaust manifold
3. Secondary throttle
4. Primary throttle
5. Carburetor
6. Preheating chamber

Emission control manifold heating system—B30 engine.

smooth if superficial, replace if burned or heat-checked

RATTLING—transmission click
    a. Release yoke and leave loose on pivot ball-stud or in bearing groove (replace if necessary)
    b. Oil in driven-disc damper (replace driven-disc
    c. Driven-disc damper spring failure (replace driven-disc)

THROW-OUT BEARING NOISE—clutch fully engaged
    a. Improper linkage adjustment
    b. Throw-out bearing binding on transmission bearing retainer (clean, lubricate, check for burrs, nicks)
    c. Insufficient tension between release yoke and pivot ball-stud (yoke improperly installed and/or linkage spring weak)

TIGHT PEDAL—when depressed or returns sluggishly
    a. Bind in linkage (lubricate and free up)
    b. Weak pressure plate spring
    c. Weak linkage spring
    d. Driven disc worn

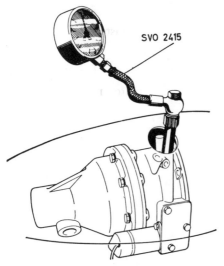

SVO 2415

Checking overdrive oil pressure through access hole.

Transmission Troubleshooting

NOISE—in forward speeds
    a. Low lubricant level or incorrect lubricant

    b. Transmission misaligned or loose
    c. Mainshaft bearing or front main bearing worn or damaged
    d. Countergear or bearings worn or damaged
    e. Main drive gear or synchronizers worn or damaged

NOISE—in reverse
    a. Reverse sliding gear or shaft, worn or damaged

HARD SHIFTING
    a. Clutch improperly adjusted
    b. Shift shafts or forks worn
    c. Incorrect lubricant
    d. Synchronizers worn or broken

JUMPING OUT OF GEAR
    a. Partial engagement of gear
    b. Transmission misaligned or loose
    c. Worn pilot bearing
    d. End play in main drive gear (bearing retainer loose or broken, loose or worn bearings on main drive gear and mainshaft)
    e. Worn clutch teeth on main drive gear and/or on synchronizer sleeve
    f. Worn or broken blocking rings
    g. Bent mainshaft

STICKING IN GEAR
    a. Clutch not released fully
    b. Low lubricant level or incorrect lubrication
    c. Defective (tight) main drive gear pilot bearing
    d. Frozen blocking ring on main drive gear cone
    e. Burred or battered teeth on synchronizer sleeve and/or main drive gear

Overdrive Troubleshooting

If faulty operation should be experienced with the transmission overdrive it may be due to a clogged oil strainer, improper overdrive pump pressure or defective control valve performance.

The following tests should help locate the trouble: The oil strainer should be cleaned at every oil change. Drain oil by removing plug marked "drain" under the oil strainer. Remove cover. Take out oil strainer and magnetic washers, clean with gasoline and blow dry with compressed air. Check that oil strainer gasket is in good condition, insert in position with steel-covered side toward housing. Install oil strainer, washers, new cover gasket and cover.

Oil Pressure Check

Disengage overdrive to remove residual pressure. Remove plug over control valve and connect gauge SVO 2415. Allow spring, tappet and ball to remain in position. Start engine and drive car. At a speed of 31-37 mph on overdrive, the gauge should show a reading of 500-570 lbs./sq. in (35–40 kg/cm²). If reading is low, first change spring and relief valve plunger. Then, if necessary, place washers under spring. (.004" alters pressure about 14.22 lbs/sq in). Trouble can also be due to worn pump parts.

Checking Oil Pump

Switch out overdrive to remove any residual oil pressure. Jack up vehicle and place blocks under front and rear axles. Remove drain plug and drain oil into a container. Remove plug under oil pump and take out the spring and ball. Remove valve seating with key SVO 2419. Clean and inspect parts. Check with a piece of wire or something similar held against the pump plunger that the pump works when the output shaft is rotated. (Turn engine over a few times with overdrive switched in and ignition coil disconnected.) The pump plunger stroke

should be .157" (4 mm). If it is shorter, the pump must be removed and the trouble ascertained.

Remove pump by removing bolt which holds pump. Attach puller SVO 2418 into the place of the valve seating and pull out pump. Disassemble pump and check parts. Assemble in reverse order.

Checking Control Valve

Jack up vehicle and place blocks under front and rear axles. Remove cover from over control valve arm. Switch in overdrive (with engine stopped and shift lever in 4th speed). If control valve is properly adjusted, it should be possible to pass a ³⁄₁₆" diameter pin through the hole in the arm and into the housing. If not, adjust until correct position is obtained.

Check current through solenoid with overdrive in. Current should be about one ampere max. If current is 10-12 amp or higher, the control solenoid does not go in far enough to cut off the control current. Determine reason and adjust. Otherwise solenoid will be damaged.

CLEANING CONTROL VALVE

Remove plug over control valve as well as spring, tappet, ball and valve rod. Lift ball with loop of wire and valve rod with a pointed wood probe pushed into opening. Clean parts. Clean valve rod with 3.1 mm drill and valve hole with a 1.1 mm drill. Assemble parts in reverse order to above.

Drive Shaft Troubleshooting

Defects in the drive shaft or drive shaft components are usually evidenced by vibration, thumping or clicking sounds. Vibration shows up as a growling noise which becomes louder as the speed increases and may be due to wear, a bent drive shaft, insufficient lubrication or improper assembly. No attempt should be made to repair a bent or damaged drive shaft. A new one should be installed as described in Chapter Eight. Worn universal joints usually cause a loud clicking sound if the car is driven slowly and speed is accelerated and decelerated. Replacement of universal joints and other parts are described also in Chapter Eight.

Removing overdrive oil pump valve seat.

Front End Troubleshooting

When servicing steering and front suspension assemblies, it is advisable to check every front end part because all of the assemblies are so closely interrelated.

First, check the front end for worn or loose-fitting parts. Repair or replace what is faulty. Second, inspect and adjust the steering gear assembly. Third, set the front end alignment. And last, balance the wheels.

To detect front-end troubles quickly, follow these simple procedures:

1. With the front end jacked up, shake both wheels simultaneously to detect any looseness between them. Tie-rod and steering linkage joints sometimes loosen under severe road stresses. Check weaknesses further by oscillating and prying against members connected to these joints.

2. Check out wheel suspension joints by having each wheel shaken up and down while the steering knuckle and control arm joints are observed for play.

3. Spin the wheels rapidly to test for deteriorated bearings. Listen for bearing noise and touch the bumper to feel vibration that rough bearings create.

4. Rig a piece of chalk so it just clears the wheel rim and rotate the wheel to test for wheel runout. The chalk will mark misaligned, protruding rim areas. Repeat test on inside rim. Wheel should be straightened if runout exceeds ⅛ inch.

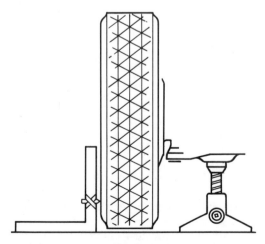

Testing for front wheel runout.

5. Lower front end to ground and rebound fenders to check for deteriorated shock absorbers.

6. Check pre-owned cars for possible front end damage by measuring and comparing the wheelbase on both sides. Measure carefully from common points such as from the rear of the front-wheel rim to the rear of the back-wheel rim. If one side has a shorter or longer wheelbase than is listed in specifications, compare several measurements on both sides between various points until the dislocated part is found.

Diagonal measurements from right front to left rear wheels and from left front to right rear wheels will uncover a distorted chassis (if wheelbase measurements are equal). A twisted chassis will alter tracking and make front end alignment difficult if not impossible.

Vehicle Wandering

Vehicle wandering requires constant steering wheel correction, is annoying and also dangerous. It may be caused by incorrect caster or toe-in, too low tire pressure, excessive or insufficient play in the steering mechanism, worn or stiff steering rod ball joints, stiff control arm system, excessive play in rear end suspension.

Pulling to One Side

Check for uneven tire pressure, weak or uneven front springs, stiff wheel bearing, faulty wheel alignment, dragging brake, bent steering rod, or incorrect camber.

Hard Steering

Caused by too-low tire pressure, insufficiently lubricated steering gears or front end, excessive caster, damaged bearing in gear housing or steering column, damaged thrust bearing in steering knuckles, damaged front axle member or body.

Shimmy

Look for bent, misaligned or unbalanced wheels, worn or warped brake drum, too-low tire pressure, damaged steering rod, loose or worn front wheel bearings.

Front End Alignment

Front end alignment centers on the precise geometric relationship of a number of

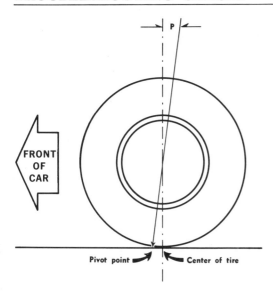

Front wheel caster. P = positive caster. The pivot point ahead of the center line of the tire holds the wheel stable.

parts—even when they are changing positions—that provides front wheel stability and control. These geometric angles include steering axis cant, caster, camber, included angle, toe-in, and toe-out (turning arc).

Before any adjustment is made, the condition of the complete front end system should be checked following the procedures given in the previous paragraphs and any defects corrected. Check the air pressure in all the tires. Check that the front tires are worn evenly. If not, replace or rotate them with the rear tires. Front wheel alignment must always be adjusted in this order: 1. Caster; 2. Camber; and 3. Toe-In.

CASTER

Caster is the cant of the upper ball joint toward the rear of the car (positive). It gives the wheel another type of directional stability by moving the pivot point of the wheel forward of the tire's center. Positioning the pivot point ahead of center causes a drag on the bottom of the wheel (at the center) when it turns, thereby resisting the turn and tending to hold the wheel steady in whatever direction it has been going. The same principle of drag holds a weather vane pointer into the wind. The vane's bulky part seeks the

point of minimum resistance behind the pivot.

Too slight a caster angle will cause the wheels to wander or weave at high speed and steer erratically when the brakes are applied. Too great a caster angle creates hard steering and shimmy at low speeds.

CAMBER

Camber is the angle that the centerline of the wheel makes with the vertical. The top of the wheel cants away from the car so that the center of the tire at the road lies at a point projected along the inclined axis of the upper and lower ball joints (steering axis cant). Placing the weight of the car directly over the pivot point allows easiest steering and takes some load off the outside wheel bearing.

TOE-OUT

Toe-out (turning arc) is the difference in angle of the two wheels in a turn. As the front end turns, the outside wheel describes a larger circle than does the inside wheel. The turning angle of each is, therefore, not the same and the difference of the two angles is toe-out. If all previously discussed front end angles and measurements are correct and yet toe-out is wrong, one or both of the steering arms are bent.

TOE-IN

Usually measured in inches, this is the amount that both wheels are closer together at the front than at the rear. Toe-in is related to wheel camber and compres-

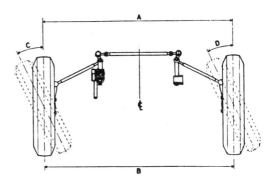

Toe-in = X−Y.

Adjusting caster and camber (144). A=Shims.

sion forces on the steering linkage with forward speed. The greater the camber, the greater is the toe-in, usually. Set toe-in only after checking caster and camber.

STEERING AXIS CANT

Steering axis cant, or kingpin inclination as termed years ago when kingpins were standard, is the angle (from the vertical) at which the steering knuckle is attached to the upper and lower ball joints. The canted steering knuckle controls wheel directional stability by forcing the wheel to lift the chassis in order to turn from a straight ahead direction. As the steering

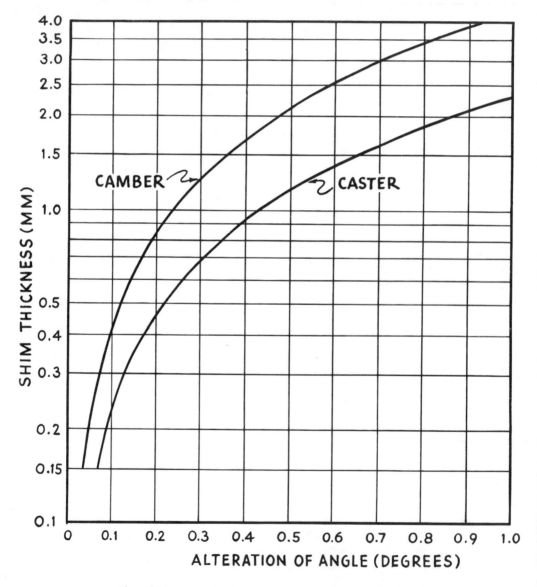

Shim thickness vs change of caster and camber angles (144).

arm releases its force over the wheel, the wheel returns to its straight ahead position under the force of the chassis weight. This inclination is not adjustable.

INCLUDED ANGLE

This is found by adding the steering axis cant to the positive wheel camber. This total must be equal on both front wheels regardless of what individual differences exist in axis cant and camber between the wheels. If the included angles of the two sides are different, a wheel spindle might be bent, possibly from striking a curb sharply.

Caster Adjustment (164, 145, 144, 1800, 122)

The caster should be 0° to + 1° and is adjusted by inserting or removing shims at the upper control arm shaft. Loosen the bolts several turns using SVO 2713, one end of which is used for the front bolt and the other for the rear bolt. Insert or remove shims as required.

Caster is increased toward the *positive* side either by inserting shims at the rear bolt, or by removing shims from the front bolt. For correct camber, the caster should be adjusted by transferring one-half the shim thickness (shown in diagram) from one bolt to the other, or simply by removing from one of the bolt positions the thickness indicated.

Tighten bolts before each measurement is made. When adjustment is complete, tighten bolts to a torque of 35–40 lb. ft.

Caster Adjustment (PV 444, 445, 544, P 122, 210)

The caster should be −¾° to +¼° and is adjusted by loosening the clamp bolt and turning the eccentric bushing with wrench SVO 1411 (early production) or wrench SVO 2201 (late production). One complete turn alters the caster angle by ½°. NOTE: if the wheel has the correct camber, one complete turn is necessary, otherwise the camber will be altered. Tighten clamp bolt each time before measuring caster.

Camber Adjustment (164, 145, 144, 1800, 122)

The camber should be 0° to +½° and is adjusted by use of shims in the upper control arm shaft. Loosen bolts a few turns with SVO 2713, one end of the wrench

1. Clamp bolt   2. Eccentric

Adjusting caster and camber (PV544).

being used for the front bolt and the other for the rear bolt. Then increase or decrease the number of shims equally at both the bolts. Camber positive angle is increased by removing shims and the negative angle increased by inserting shims. After each adjustment, tighten bolts before checking.

Camber Adjustment (PV 444, 445, 544, P 210)

After caster has been checked, camber can be adjusted to proper angle of −¼° to +½° by loosening the clamp bolt and turning the eccentric with wrench SVO 1411 or SVO 2201. An alteration of camber causes a slight but negligible change in caster.

Toe-In Adjustment

Toe-in should be 5⁄32″ and is adjusted by loosening the clamp bolts on the tie rod, and turning the rod in the required direction. Toe-in is increased by turning the rod in the direction of forward wheel rotation. Check caster and camber before adjusting toe-in.

King-Pin Inclination

King-pin inclination should be checked and should be 5° when the camber is 0°.

Wheel Balance

Front end alignment will not remain correct long if wheels are not balanced both dynamically and statically. See Chapter 1, under *Wheel and Tire Care*.

Chassis and Wheel Alignment Specifications

Model	Chassis		Wheel Alignment				Wheel Pivot Ratio	
	Wheelbase (In.)	Track (In.)	Caster (Deg.)	Camber (Deg.)	Toe-In (In.)	King Pin Inclin. (Deg.)	Inner	Outer
PV444, PV445, PV544	102.5	51.0(F), 51.7(R)	-3/4 to +1/4	-1/4 to + 1/2	0 to .118	5	22 ±1	20
122	102.4	51.7	0 to +1	0 to +1/2	0 to .154	8		
142, 144, 145	102.4	53.1	0 to +1	0 to +1/2	0 to .16	7.5	21.5 to 23.5	20
164	106.3	53.2	0 to +1	0 to +1/2	0 to .16	7.5	21.5 to 23.5	20

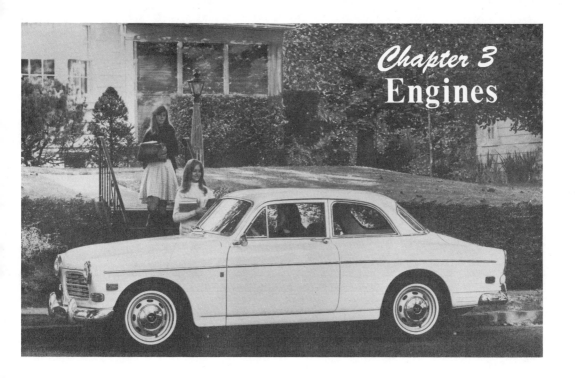

Chapter 3
Engines

Description

Volvo engines B14, B16, B18 and B20 are all four cylinder, water-cooled, overhead-valve, engines. The B30 is similar to the earlier series, differing mainly by having six cylinders. The B14 engine was superceded in 1958 by the B16 engine. The B18 engine was introduced in 1962 and the B20 in 1968. The B30, used in the 164, was introduced in 1969.

B18, B20 and B30 Engines

The B18 series of engines consists of Models B18A, B18B and B18 D. The B18A is provided with a Zenith 36VN down draft carburetor (some production models were provided with a horizontal Zenith-Stromberg 175CD2S), while the B18B and B18D models both have either twin Zenith-Stromberg 175-2SE or twin Horizontal SU-HS6 types. SAE bhp outputs are 75 @ 4500 rpm for the B18A; 100 @ 5500 for the B18B; and 90 @ 5000 for the B18D. B18B engines incorporate an oil cooler, positive crankcase ventilation and other design features not included on the B18A.

The B20 series consists of the B20A and B20B engines. The B20A, not imported to the U.S., has a single Zenith-Stromberg 175-CD-2SE carburetor, and the B20B, imported to the U.S., has either two Zenith-Stromberg 175-CD-2SE or two SU-HS6 carburetors. The B30 engine is equipped with two Zenith-Stromberg 175-CD-2SE carburetors.

The cylinder block is a single unit made of cast iron alloy. The machined cylinder bores are surrounded by cooling jackets. Oil openings are arranged so that the full-flow oil filter (with the oil cooler in B18B engines) is attached directly to the right side of the block.

The cylinder head is bolted to the block. All combustion chambers are machined with intake and exhaust valve ports and cooling water jackets. The overhead valves are made of special steel with chrome stems and are mounted in replaceable guides.

The crankshaft is drop forged steel with drilled oil ways and case hardened crankpins. There are five main bearings on the B18 and B20, seven on the B30, the rear bearing also functioning as a thrust bearing. The main bearings and bearing inserts of the B18, B20 and B30 engines are steel-backed, indium-plated lead bronze. Bearing inserts can be replaced without removing the engine.

A camshaft of special alloy cast iron and case hardened cams is driven from the crankshaft through a gear train which has a reduction ratio of 2:1. The camshaft is guided axially by a thrust washer at the front end. A shim behind the camshaft gear determines the clearance. Valve lifters are actuated directly by the camshaft. They are located in the block above the camshaft and transfer movement to the valves by means of push rods and rocker arms. There are no inspection covers for the valve lifters since they are accessible from above when the cylinder head is removed.

Connecting rods of drop forged steel are provided with precision-machined bushings which act as bearings for the wrist pins. Bearing inserts are replaceable. Pistons are made of light alloy and have two compression rings and one oil ring. The upper compression ring is chrome to reduce cylinder wear. The wrist pins are floating in both the piston and connecting rod. Axial movement of the wrist pin is limited by circlips in the wrist pin hole.

The engine employs a forced-feed lubricating system, pressure being provided by a pump driven by the camshaft and located in the oil pan under the crankshaft. The pump forces oil past a relief valve on the pump, through the oil filter and through oil passages to various lubricating points. All oil supplied to lubricating points, therefore, first passes through the oil filter.

The oil pump is a gear type. The pressure pipe from the pump to the cylinder block has no threads but is tightened in position when the pump bolts are secured. There are special rubber seals at each end of the pipe. The relief valve is mounted directly on the pump.

The oil filter is a full-flow type and on B18, B20 and B30 engines is mounted directly on the cylinder block. (On the B18B, an oil cooler is installed between the oil filter and the cylinder block. This is described in a later paragraph.) The filter element is made of special paper and should be replaced when it becomes dirty.

General Engine Specifications

Type	Cu. In. Displacement (cc's)	Carburetion	SAE Horsepower @ rpm	Torque (ft. lbs.) @ rpm	Bore x Stroke (in.)	Compress. Ratio	Normal Oil Pressure (psi)
B-14A	86 (1410)	Dual Sidedraft	70 @ 5,500	75.9 @ 3,000	2.953 x 3.150	7.8:1	43–57 @ 2,000
B-16A	96.4 (1580)	Single Downdraft	66 @ 4,500	86.5 @ 2,500	3.125 x 3.150	7.4:1	36–50 @ 2,000
B-16B	96.4 (1580)	Dual Sidedraft	85 @ 5,500	87 @ 3,500	3.125 x 3.150	8.2:1	36–50 @ 2,000
B-16D	96.4 (1580)		72 @ 5,500	86.1 @ 2,600	3.125 x 3.150	8.2:1	36–50 @ 2,000
B-18A	109 (1780)	Single Downdraft	75 @ 4,500	103 @ 2,800	3.313 x 3.150	8.5:1	50–85 @ 2,000
B-18B	109 (1780)	Dual Sidedraft	100 @ 5,500	108 @ 4,000	3.313 x 3.150	9.5:1	50–85 @ 2,000
B-18D	109 (1780)	Dual Sidedraft	90 @ 5,000	105 @ 3,500	3.313 x 3.150	8.5:1	50–85 @ 2,000
B-20A	122 (1990)	Single Sidedraft	90 @ 4,800	119 @ 3,000	3.50 x 3.150	8.7:1	36–85 @ 2,000
B-20B	122 (1990)	Dual Sidedraft	118 @ 5,800	123 @ 3,500	3.50 x 3.150	9.5:1	36–85 @ 2,000
B-30A	183 (2980)	Dual Sidedraft	145 @ 5,500	163 @ 3,000	3.50 x 3.150	9.2:1	36–85 @ 2,000

The oil filter contains a valve which allows oil to bypass the element if resistance to flow becomes excessive.

The oil cooler on B18B engines is installed between the oil filter and cylinder block and consists of an oil duct surrounded by a water cooling jacket. Baffles in the paths of the oil and cooling water conduct heat away from the oil.

The B18, B20 and B30 engines are equipped with positive crankcase ventilation, which prevents crankcase gases from being released into the atmosphere. Instead the gases are sucked into the combustion chambers of the engine through the intake manifold. Between the crankcase and intake manifold, there is a connection which consists of two rubber hoses and an oil trap attached to the valve inspection cover. One of the hoses contains a valve and is connected between the oil trap and the intake manifold. The valve controls the flow of gases sucked into the intake manifold from the crankcase and also acts as a check valve to prevent carburetor backfire from reaching the crankcase. The other hose is connected between the oil filler cap on the rocker arm casing and the carburetor air filter and supplies fresh filtered air to the crankcase. The oil filler cap has a built in flame trap which, like the control valve, prevents backfire from reaching the rocker arm casing. At full engine load, when the partial vacuum in the crankcase is less than that in the air filter, air flow from the filter to the rocker arm casing reverses and crankcase gases then go through both hoses to the intake manifold. Thus, the PCV can handle relatively large volumes of crankcase gas.

The distributor which is driven by a bevel gear from the crankshaft has both a centrifugal and vacuum regulator. The direction of rotation is counterclockwise and the firing order is 1-3-4-2 for the B18 and B20, 1-5-3-6-2-4 for the B30.

B14 and B16 Engines

This series of engines consists of Models B14A, B16A, B16B and B16D. The B14A is equipped with twin SU-H2 horizontal carburetors, while the B16A and B16D each have a single Zenith 34VN down draft carburetor. The B16B is equipped with twin SU-H4 horizontal carburetors which are somewhat larger than those on the B14A. SAE bhp outputs are 70 @ 5500 rpm for the B14A; 66 @ 4500 for the B16A; 85 @ 5500 for the B15B; and 72 @ 5500 for the B16D.

The cylinder block is a single unit made of cast iron alloy. The machined cylinder bores are surrounded by cooling jackets. Oil openings are arranged in the B16A, B16B and B16D blocks so that the oil filter is attached directly to the side of the engine. The oil filter on B14A engines is connected to the engine by external lines. The crankshaft is drop forged steel with case hardened crankpins. There are three main bearings, the rear bearing also functioning as a thrust bearing. Undersize inserts are available to provide the correct clearance for reground journals, and bearing inserts can be replaced without removing the engine. The main bearings and connecting rod bearings (except on the B16A) are steel-backed, indium-plated lead bronze. On the B16A engine, connecting rod bearings are special lead-bronze alloy, while the main bearings are babbit lined. A camshaft of special steel with hardened cams is guided axially by a thrust washer at the front end.

Pistons are made of light alloy and have two compression rings and one oil ring. The upper compression ring is chrome to reduce cylinder wear. Pistons contain a stamping on the top to indicate direction of installation. Connecting rods of drop forged steel are provided with precision-machined bearings and bushings. Bearing inserts are replaceable. The wrist pins are floating in both the piston and connecting rod. Axial movement of the wrist pin is limited by circlips in the wrist pin hole.

The engine employs a forced feed lubricating system, pressure being supplied by a pump driven by the camshaft. The pump forces oil first through the filter and then through oil passages to the various points. On the B16 engines, the oil filter is attached directly to the side of the block. The B14A oil filter is connected to the oil system by external lines. The filter element is made of special paper and should be replaced when it becomes dirty. A valve in the oil filter allows oil to bypass the element if resistance to flow becomes excessive. The distributor which is driven by a bevel gear from the crankshaft has both a centrifugal and vacuum regulator. Ignition timing on the B14A engine can be retarded or advanced by a screw adjustment on the distributor. The direction of rotation is counterclockwise and the firing order is 1-3-4-2. Top dead center is indicated by markings on the flywheel and pulley, and a raised spot on the timing gear casing.

Engine Components and Assemblies

The following paragraphs give procedures for removal of engine components and assemblies for repair or replacement without removing the engine from the vehicle.

Water Pump Replacement

1. Drain the cooling system by opening one drain cock on the radiator and one on the rear right side of the engine.

2. Loosen the fan belt by loosening the generator mounting bolts, and disconnect the water pipes.

3. Remove the pump, noting the position of the sealing rings on top of the pump so that they can be replaced in the same position.

4. Before installing new pump, make sure the sealing rings are in good condition and are pushed into the pipe thoroughly. Press the pump upward against the cylinder head extension while bolting into position so that there is a good seal.

5. Fill the cooling system and test run the engine for leakage.

Thermostat Replacement

Remove the bolts from the flange in the upper water line which houses the thermostat, and turn the pipe up and out of the way. Replace the thermostat using a new gasket. Position the water pipe, install the bolts and fill cooling system. Check for leaks.

Oil Filter Replacement

The oil filter is screwed onto a nipple in the block on B18A, B20 and B30 engines. On B18B engines, it screws onto a nipple in the air cooler.

B18, B20 and B30 Engines

Remove the old filter by turning with the hands or with a chain wrench. Discard old filter. Coat the rubber gasket of the new filter with oil and make sure both contacting surfaces are clean. Screw on the filter by hand until it just comes to the end of its travel. Then screw in the filter a further half-turn by hand. *Do not use the chain wrench for tightening the filter.* Start engine and check for oil leaks.

B16 Engines

Loosen the center bolt on the oil filter housing, being prepared to collect the oil that runs out. Remove the oil filter. Discard the old element and clean the filter housing. Insert the new element (observing the "up" marking) and gasket in the housing, and bolt filter unit to side of engine, guiding it with the hand so that it fits into the groove correctly. Tighten bolt to torque of 15 lb. ft. (2 kgm). Add 1½ pints of oil to the crankcase for the new filter element. Start the engine and check for oil leaks.

B14 Engines

Drain filter by removing oil plug from the side of the filter support. Loosen center bolt on oil filter housing and remove filter. Discard old filter element and clean filter housing. Install new filter element. Install drain plug and attached oil filter assembly to support. Add 1½ pints of oil to crankcase for new filter element. Run engine and check for oil leaks.

Removing oil filter.

B18B Engines

Drain cooling system. Disconnect water connection from oil cooler. Remove oil filter. Unscrew nut on oil nipple and remove the oil cooler. The O-ring may require replacement, in which case the new O-ring should be inserted into the groove in the oil cooler after the groove is coated with gasket cement. Tighten the nut on the oil cooler to a torque of 7 lb. ft. (1 kgm). Check that the cooler is in good contact with block, then tighten nut to a torque of 23–25 lb.ft. (3–3.5 kgm). Install the oil filter and connect the water lines. Fill the cooling system and start the engine. Check for oil and water leaks.

Dual Carburetor Replacement

The dual carburetors both must be removed at the same time from the intake manifold since they are interconnected by an intermediate shaft. Remove the air cleaners, fuel and vacuum connections and disconnect throttle controls. Remove screws holding both carburetors to the intake manifold. Pull both carburetors off at the same time with the shaft in position. Cover the intake manifold ports with masking tape.

Replace carburetors by reversing above steps, and installing both carburetors at the same time with the intermediate shaft in position. Make necessary idling and synchronizing adjustments as described in Chapter Two.

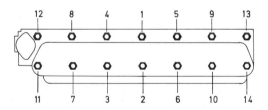

Cylinder head tightening sequence, B30 engine.

Cylinder Head Replacement

Drain the cooling system (drains front and rear). Disconnect the throttle and choke controls. Remove the carburetor. (See special instructions for dual carburetors). Disconnect the exhaust pipe at the exhaust manifold. Disconnect hoses to the radiator and other connections to the cylinder head. Loosen fan belt and remove

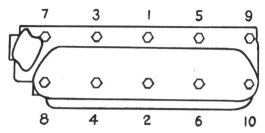

Sequence for tightening cylinder head.

rocker arm casing, rocker arm shaft and push rods. Remove cylinder head.

When installing cylinder head, . screw guide pins (SVO 2435) into the front right and left rear holes. Coat new gasket on both sides with graphite grease and lay gasket on block. Install cylinder head over the guide pins. Remove guide pins and insert bolts. Tighten bolts in the sequence illustrated, and to a torque of 61–69 lb.ft. (8.5–9.5 kgm).

Timing Gears, Camshaft Replacement

To replace the timing gears:

1. Drain the cooling system. Remove the hood and radiator.

2. Remove the fan and pulley on the water pump. Remove the crankshaft bolt, and then remove the pulley, using puller SVO 2279 (B14, B16).

3. Remove the timing gear casing. Loosen a couple of the oil pan bolts, being careful not to damage the gasket.

4. Measure tooth flank clearance. Maximum permissible gear backlash for the B14, B16, and B18 engines is 0.005 in. (0.12 mm.). For the B20 and B30 the figure is 0.0016–0.0032 in. (0.04–0.08 mm.). Also measure end play of camshaft. This is determined by a shim behind the camshaft gear. Correct values are given in the specifications.

5. Note correct relative position of gears by the markings on them. Remove the hub from the crankshaft with puller SVO 2440 for the four cylinder engines, and SVO 2814 for the B30 engine. Remove the crankshaft gear with puller SVO 2250. Pull the crankshaft gear with SVO 1428 on the B14 and B16, SVO 2405 for the B18 and B20, and SVO 2822 for the B30. Remove oil jet, blow air through it and replace it. Oil fed through this jet lubricates the gears.

6. If the camshaft is to be replaced, it will be necessary to remove the thrust

Removing camshaft gear.

SVO 2407

Installing crankshaft gear.

Removing crankshaft gear.

SVO 2408

Installing camshaft gear.

flange and the valve lifters. The camshaft can then be pulled out the front after the radiator is removed. Valve lifters can be pushed out after removal of rocker arms, push rods, fuel pump, distributor and covers on the sides of the engine.

7. Reassemble in reverse order, installing new camshaft. Install the crankshaft gear with tool SVO 2407 for the four cylinder engines, and SVO 2815 for the B30. Install the camshaft gear using tool SVO 2408, making sure the gears are in the correct relative position according to the markings. Tool SVO 2407 has flats for turning the crankshaft. Do not push the camshaft backwards, or the seal washer on the rear end may be forced out. Again check gear clearance and shaft end play.

1. Oil jet   2. Gear markings

Observe timing gear markings.

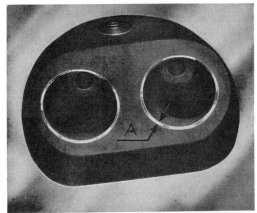

Valve seat width. A = 0.055" (1.4mm).

8. When assembling timing gear casing, make sure drain holes in casing are open and that the casing is properly centered. Center casing using sleeve SVO 2438.

Replacing Valves, De-Carbonizing

To recondition valves and guides, remove cylinder head and place it on a clean surface. Using valve spring compressor pliers, remove keys (keepers), caps and springs. Place valves in order in a stand.

Use only a soft wire brush for removing carbon to avoid scratching valve seats and valve faces. Cut a chisel from hardwood for chipping carbon from the cylinder chamber. The wood is less likely to score the metal surfaces.

Inspect valve guides. See Valve Specifications table for proper valve stem to valve guide clearance. Worn or pitted guides can be reamed to accept oversize valves. Valves are marked near the stem (NOTE: always check valve stem diameter, since oversize valves are sometimes used in production).

Grind valve seats to 45° angle. Seat width for B14, B16 and B18 engines is 0.055 in. (1.4 mm.) intake and exhaust. Seat width for B20 and B30 is 0.080 in. (2.0 mm.), intake and exhaust. If the seat is too wide after grinding, it can be reduced by using a 70° grinding stone from the inside and a 20° grinding stone from the outside. Resurface valves to 44.5°—intake and exhaust.

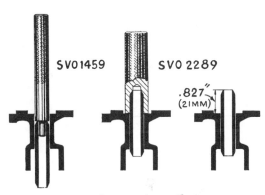

SVO1459   SVO 2289
.827"
(21MM)

Replacing valve guides.

Adjusting valve clearance.

Engine Rebuilding Specifications

Engine	Seat[1] Angle (deg.)	Seat Width (in.)	Spring Press. (psi.) @ Length (in.)	Spring Free Length (in.)	Valves Stem Diameter (in.) Intake[3]	Exhaust[3]	Stem-to-Guide Clearance (in.) Intake[2]	Exhaust[2]	Guide Height Above Head (in.)
B-14	45		145 @ 1.20	1.77	.3094-.3100	.3085-.3095	.0012-.0024	.0017-.0033	.83
B-16A	45	.060	145 @ 1.20	1.77	.3094-.3100	.3082-.3089	.0012-.0024	.0024-.0035	.83
B-16B	45	.060	145 @ 1.20	1.77	.3094-.3100	.3082-.3089	.0012-.0024	.0024-.0035	.83
B-18A	45	.055	65 @ 1.57	1.77	.3413-.3438	.3403-.3409	.0010-.0021	.0025-.0037	.83
B-18B	45	.055	65 @ 1.57	1.77	.3413-.3438	.3403-.3409	.0010-.0021	.0025-.0037	.83
B-18D	45	.055	145 @ 1.20	1.77	.3413-.3438	.3403-.3409	.0010-.0021	.0025-.0037	.83
B-20A	45	.080	65 @ 1.57	1.81	.3132-.3138	.3120-.3126	.0012-.0026	.0024-.0038	.689
B-20B	45	.080	65 @ 1.57	1.81	.3132-.3138	.3120-.3126	.0012-.0026	.0024-.0038	.689
B-30A	45	.080	56 @ 1.54	1.77	.3132-.3138	.3120-.3126	.0012-.0026	.0024-.0038	.689

[1] Valve face angle 44.5°.   [2] Maximum stem to guide clearance .006 in.   [3] Maximum valve stem wear .0008 in.

Lubricate and install. Install valve springs with closely wound end of coils toward cylinder head.

REPLACING VALVE GUIDES

Press out old valve guide on the B14, B16 and B18 using tool SVO 1459. Use tool SVO 2818 for the B20 and B30. Press in new guides in the B14, B16 and B18 using tool SVO 2289 and in the B20 and B30 using tool SVO 2819. The tool gives correct depth. Check that guides are not burred and that valves move freely in them. Check valve springs for conformance to specifications. Lubricate valves and install, fitting the lower rubber washer, steel washer (early production), valve spring, upper washer and keeper, and then rubber ring.

Valve Adjustment

Valve clearance can be adjusted whether the engine is warm or cold since it is identical although it is best to adjust valves after a road test. Adjust valves to the values shown in the table. When piston No. 1 is at TDC, valves 1, 2, 3 and 5 are adjusted, and with piston No. 4 at TDC, valves 4, 6, 7 and 8 are adjusted. For the B30, when piston No. 1 is at TDC, valves 1, 2, 3, 6, 7, and 10 are adjusted and when piston No. 6 is at TDC, valves 4, 5, 8, 9, 11, and 12 are adjusted.

Rocker Arm Replacement

Replace rocker arm bushings when wear has reached .004″ (.1 mm). Use tool SVO 1867 (SVO 4154, for B14 and B16 engines) to press out the old and insert the new bushings. Ream the new bushings to an accurate fit on the shafts. Line up the hole in the bushing with the hole in the rocker arm. If the pressure

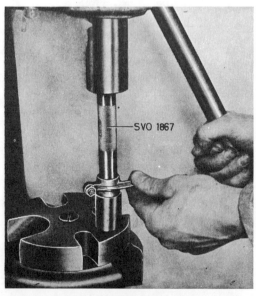

SVO 1867

Replacing rocker arm bushing.

Reaming rocker arm bushing.

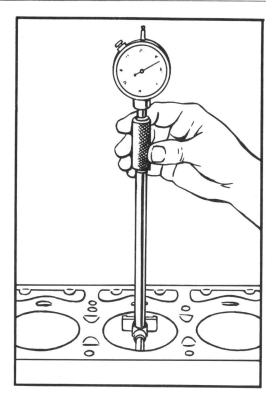

Measuring cylinder bore.

pad of the rocker arm is deformed, a special grinding machine is required since the hardened pad surface is thin.

Oil Pan Removal (B14, B16)

The oil pan can be removed from B14 and B16 engines without removing the engine from the vehicle. Drain the oil and remove the cover plates from the sides of the engine. Remove the cover from under the flywheel. Loosen the nuts on the forward engine supports for about one-inch of travel, but do not remove them completely. Jack the front end and slide one-inch (2.5 mm) spacers (SVO 4124) between the engine supports and the motor mounts, and lower the jack. Remove the bolts holding the oil pan and remove the pan by pulling it downwards and backwards. Assemble in reverse order, replacing the cork gasket if it is damaged.

Replacing Pistons, Rings, Connecting Rods

Piston rings on B14 and B16 models can be replaced as follows and without removing the engine, after the cylinder head is lifted and the engine de-carbonized as previously described. While these instructions apply also to the B18, B20 and B30, the work is more easily accomplished on these after the engine is removed from the frame.

Lift the front end of the vehicle and support it about 8″ (20 mm) above the floor. (Remove B18, B20 and B30 engine from frame as described elsewhere.) Drain crankcase and remove oil pan. Note connecting rod markings. Disconnect rods at the crankshaft, replacing bearing shells, caps and nuts on rods to avoid possible interchange of parts. Remove cylinder bore ridges with a ridge reamer and push out pistons and rods up through tops of cylinders. Mark cylinder numbers on pistons, connecting rods and caps, numbering 1 through 4 or 1 through 6. Remove rings.

Inspect cylinder walls for scoring, roughness, or ridges from excessive wear. With an accurate cylinder gauge or inside micrometer, check for cylinder taper and out-of-round at top, middle and bottom of bore, both parallel and at right angles to the center line of the engine. Wear is indicated by the difference between the highest and lowest readings. Cylinder should be rebored when wear reaches .010″ (.25 mm) or if scoring is evident. Hone or rebore for smallest possible oversize piston and rings. Obtain piston first and then rework cylinder bore to ap-

Measuring piston outer diameter.

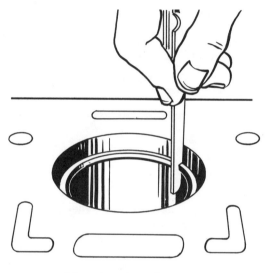

Measuring piston ring gap.

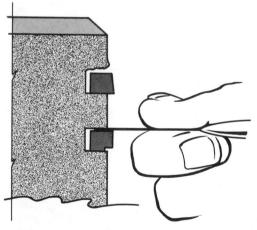

Measuring ring clearance in groove. Inspecting top ring groove for excessive wear.

propriate size. Pistons should have a clearance of .0008″–0016″ (.02–.04 mm) between piston and cylinder wall. Piston is fitted in cylinder without the rings.

Measure outside diameter of pistons with a micrometer at right angles to the wrist pin hole about ⅜″ from the bottom edge on B14A engines. This distance is ⅛″ on early production B18 engines and ½″ on late production B18 engines. On the B20 and B30 engines the distance is 0.098 in. (2.5 mm.) from the bottom.

In a new or rebored cylinder, press the rings one after another into the cylinder bore and measure the ring gap with a feeler gauge. The gap is 0.010–0.020 in. (0.25–0.50 mm.) for B14, B16, and B18 engines; 0.016–0.022 in. (0.40–0.55 mm.) for the B20 and B30 engines. If the gap is too small, widen it by filing with a thin flat file. When checking the fit in a worn cylinder bore, rings must be checked at the bottom dead center position, where the diameter of the bore is smallest.

Clean piston ring grooves and check the rings in their proper grooves in the piston. Measure the clearance at a few points as shown. See specifications for measurements. Inspect ring grooves for wear, particularly upper edge of compression ring (top) groove.

If the wrist pin hole in the piston is too worn, an oversize wrist pin is necessary. Ream out the hole to the oversize pin measurement. This is correct when the wrist pin can be pushed through the hole by hand with light resistance.

Check to see if the connecting rods are bent or twisted and straighten them if necessary. If the bushing is worn, replace it using tool SVO 1867 (SVO 1335A for B14 engines). Make sure the oil holes line up with the holes in the connecting rod, then ream the bushing to the correct fit. The wrist pin should slide through the hole with light thumb pressure but without noticeable looseness.

When assembling, be sure that the piston is positioned in the cylinder so that the arrow (or slot) faces forward. This is important since the hole is not centered in the piston, and if the piston is turned the wrong way it will cause a loud noise. Also, the connecting rod should be positioned so that the number on the side faces away from the camshaft side. Use a piston ring

Special tool for inserting piston, SVO 2176, SVO 2278, or SVO 2229.

expander tool to install the rings. Position them so the gaps do not come directly under each other. The upper piston ring is chrome, and the upper side is marked "TOP".

Lubricate the pistons, wrist pins and cylinder walls and install pistons in cylinders. Use fitting ring SVO 2176 for B18, SVO 2278 for B16 and SVO 2229 for B14 engines. Use fitting ring SVO 2823 for B20 and B30 engines.

Install the connecting rods on the crankshaft. Tighten connecting rod bolts with a torque wrench to the torque shown in the specifications.

Replacing Main Bearings

The main bearing shells can be replaced on B14 and B16 engines after dropping the oil pan and without removing the engines from the frame. In B18, B20 and B30 engines replacement of main bearing shells is best accomplished after removing the engine from the vehicle. After this is done, and the oil pan is dropped these same instructions apply:

Remove the lockwashers, nuts and bolts from the bearings. Remove the bearing caps and lower bearing inserts. Remove the upper bearing insert by placing a pin

in the oil hole and turning the crankshaft. This moves the bearing shell so that it can be removed from the crankshaft.

Rotate and inspect crankshaft journals. If out-of-roundness is more than .002″ (.05 mm), or they are scored or ridged, the crankshaft should be removed and reground. Slight roughness may be polished out with fine pumice polishing cloth saturated with engine oil.

Inspect bearings. Also check for proper bearing clearance. Clearance cannot be adjusted—new bearings must be installed. They are available in standard and undersizes. Never file ends of bearing shells to make a closer fit.

Coat with engine oil and install new bearing shells. Make sure the keys are correctly lodged. Install bearing caps with bolts and new lock washers. Tighten bolts to a torque of 87–94 lb.ft. (12–13 kgm) for big end bearings.

Engine Removal

The Volvo engine and transmission are removed from the chassis as a unit. A lifting tool (SVO 4118 for B14 and B16, SVO 2425 for B18, SVO 2869, 2870 and 2810 for B20, and SVO 2810, 2811 and 2812 for B30) is an aid. Proceed as follows:

1. Drain the oil and the cooling system. Remove hood, air cleaners, battery and radiator. Disconnect fuel line from fuel pump.

2. Disconnect throttle, choke controls, ignition, starter and generator cables. Disconnect the exhaust pipe at the exhaust manifold and the attachment on the flywheel housing.

3. Place the gear shift in neutral and remove the gear shift lever. Cover the transmission.

4. Jack vehicle to one foot height above floor and block it. Disconnect clutch return spring and controls, speedometer cable, overdrive and backup light cables.

5. Disconnect driveshaft from transmission. Remove the nuts from the engine mounting bolts. Place a jack under the transmission. Lift it slightly and remove the supporting cross-member. Remove the brackets for the exhaust manifold and rear engine mounting.

Engine Rebuilding Specifications

Engine Model	Bore		Pistons*		Rings		
	Standard Size (in.)	Maximum Wear (in.)	Piston-to-Bore Clearance (in.)	Wrist Pin [1] Diameter (in.), fit	End Gap (in.)	Oil Ring Side Clearance (in.)	Compression Ring Side Clearance (in.)
B-14	2.9512-2.9516	.010	.0016-.0024		.010-.020	.0017-.0028	.0027-.0031
B-16A	3.1248-3.1252	.010	.0012-.0020	.748, floating	.010-.020	.0017-.0028	.0027-.0031
B-16B	3.1248-3.1252	.010	.0012-.0020	.748, floating	.010-.020	.0017-.0028	.0027-.0031
B-18A	3.313	.010	.0008-.0016	.866, floating	.010-.020	.0017-.0028	.0021-.0032
B-18B	3.313	.010	.0008-.0016	.866, floating	.010-.020	.0017-.0028	.0021-.0032
B-18D	3.313	.010	.0008-.0016	.866, floating	.010-.020	.0017-.0028	.0021-.0032
B-20A	3.500	.010	.0008-.0016	.866, floating	.016-.022	.0017-.0028	.0017-.0028
B-20B	3.500	.010	.0008-.0016	.866, floating	.016-.022	.0017-.0028	.0017-.0028
B-30A	3.500	.010	.0008-.0016	.866, floating	.016-.022	.0017-.0028	.0017-.0028

[1] Wrist pin pressed into connecting rod, slide fit in piston.
* Maximum piston weight deviation − .35 oz. (10 g.).

Engine Rebuilding Specifications

Engine Model	Crankshaft								
	Main Bearing Journals (in.)					Connecting Rod Bearing Journals (in.)			
	Journal Diameter					Journal Diameter			
	Standard Size	Max. out of Rd.	Oil Clearance	Shaft [1] end-play	Thrust on No.	Standard Size	Max. out of Rd.	Oil Clearance	End-play
B-16A	2.1240-2.1244	.002	.0005-.0025	.0004-.0040	rear	1.8736-1.8740	.003	.0020-.0036	.006-.014
B-16B	2.1240-2.1244	.002	.0005-.0025	.0004-.0040	rear	1.8736-1.8740	.003	.0020-.0034	.006-.014
B-18A	2.4977-2.4982	.002	.001-.003	.0007-.0042	rear	2.1295-2.1300	.003	.0015-.0032	.006-.014
B-18B	2.4977-2.4982	.002	.0015-.0035	.0007-.0042	rear	2.1295-2.1300	.003	.0015-.0032	.006-.014
B-18D	2.4977-2.4982	.002	.001-.003	.0007-.0042	rear	2.1295-2.1300	.003	.0015-.0032	.006-.014
B-20A	2.4977-2.4982	.002	.001-.003	.0007-.0042	rear	2.1295-2.1300	.0028	.0015-.0032	.006-.014
B-20B	2.4977-2.4982	.002	.001-.003	.0007-.0042	rear	2.1295-2.1300	.0028	.0015-.0032	.006-.014
B-30A	2.4977-2.4982	.002	.0015-.0035	.0019-.0054	rear	2.1295-2.1300	.0028	.0015-.0035	.006-.014

[1] Maximum end-play .006 in.

6. Attach lifting chain SVO 4118 (B14 and B16 engines) and lift engine from vehicle by lifting front end first.

7. On B18 engines, attach lifting tool SVO 2425 to engine by installing tool bolt in fuel line clamp bolt-hole on the front end of the cylinder head, and placing the hooks under the front and rear ends of the manifold. Lift out engine front first.

Engine Disassembly

After the engine has been removed, place it in a stand and allow excess oil to drain. Using small quantities of solvent, remove dirt and grease, cleaning small areas of the engine at a time. Flush with hot water and blow engine dry with compressed air.

Remove transmission. Remove spark plugs, generator, starter and cover plates on the lower front edge of the flywheel housing. Remove the clutch and flywheel. The clutch, flywheel and crankshaft have been balanced as a unit, so mark these components so that they may be replaced in the same position. Remove the rear sealing flange, being careful not to damage the contact surfaces. Remove the water pump, distributor, rocker arm housing, thermostat housing, and intake and exhaust manifolds. Remove the rocker arms, cylinder head, oil filter (and oil cooler on B18B models). Remove the valve lifters with tool SVO 2424 (B18).

Remove the timing gear housing, timing gears and camshaft. Place engine on end and support with blocks so that crankshaft can rotate freely. Remove oil pan, oil pump, connecting rods and pistons. Number pistons one through four. Replace caps on respective connecting rods.

Turn engine upside down, support, and remove crankshaft. Replace caps correctly.

Cleaning

Clean dismantled steel or cast iron parts in a degreasing tank. Never wash light alloy parts such as pistons and bearing shells in caustic solutions. Clean them with mild soap and warm water and dry them with compressed air. Remove oil seals and clean all oil openings in block. Blow air through them.

Cylinder Reboring

Sophisticated machinery is required to rebore the cylinders so that they are at right angles to the crankshaft within very close tolerances, perfectly circular and without taper throughout their length. After reboring, cylinders are honed to a very high finish to achieve precise ring-to-wall seal and the shortest engine "break-in" time.

The rebored cylinder block should be washed in a degreasing tank before assembly in order to remove grinding residue and other foreign matter. See "Pistons, Rings, Connecting Rods" for information on making measurements and fitting pistons.

Crankshaft Grinding

Measure each crankshaft journal with a micrometer at several points around the circumference and along the axis. Taper should not exceed .002" (.05 mm). Out-of-roundness of main bearing journals should not exceed .002" and .003" (.07 mm) on the connecting rod bearing journals. Place the crankshaft on V-blocks and rotate it with a micrometer gauge against the center main bearing journal to check that it is straight within .002" (.05 mm). The crankshaft can be straightened in a press. When these limits are exceeded, the crankshaft should be ground to undersize in a special machine. If crankshaft is distorted, straighten it before grinding.

Grinding of the journals must be carried out to the measurements given in the specifications so that the available undersize bearing shells will fit properly. Main and connecting rod bearing journals are ground to identical measurements. The fillets at the ends of the journals should have a radius of .080–.100" (2.0–2.5 mm). After grinding, burrs should be carefully removed from all oil openings, the crankshaft fine-ground to a polish and thoroughly cleaned before assembly.

Oil Seal Replacement

The rear main bearing has an oil seal which is held in place by a flange and washer. Make sure the seal is in good condition and that the flange is clean. Check that the drain hole is not blocked by improper fitting of the oil pan gasket. To reassemble, install seal and flange but do

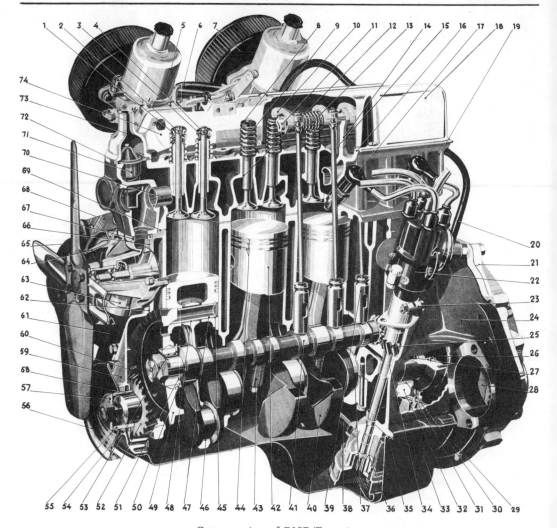

Cutaway view of B18B/D engine.

1. Upper valve washer
2. Exhaust valve
3. Valve cotter
4. Inlet valve
5. Front carburetor
6. Fuel hose
7. Rear air cleaner
8. Sealing ring
9. Valve spring
10. Rocker arm
11. Rocker arm shaft
12. Valve guide
13. Spring
14. Bearing block
15. Pushrod
16. Rocker arm casing gasket
17. Cable terminal on spark plug
18. Rocker arm casing
19. Cylinder head
20. Vacuum hose
21. Flywheel housing
22. Distributor
23. Clamp
24. Cylinder block
25. Distributor drive gear

26. Circlip and washer
27. Pilot bearing
28. Flywheel
29. Cover plate
30. Flange bearing shell
31. Sealing flange
32. Main bearing cap
33. Oil pan
34. Bushing
35. Gasket
36. Oil pump
37. Main bearing shell
38. Oil delivery pipe
39. Valve tappet
40. Crankshaft
41. Camshaft
42. Piston
43. Connecting rod
44. Piston rings
45. Circlip
46. Big-end bearing shell
47. Wrist pin
48. Wrist pin bushing
49. Camshaft gear
50. Thrust washer

51. Spacing ring
52. Crankshaft gear
53. Key
54. Seat
55. Hub
56. Belt pulley
57. Washer
58. Key
59. Timing gear casing
60. Oil jet
61. Water inlet
62. Gasket
63. Water pump
64. Belt pulley
65. Generator
66. Gasket
67. Sealing ring
68. Belt tensioner
69. Cylinder head gasket
70. Distributor pipe
71. Thermostat
72. Gasket
73. Water inlet
74. Intake manifold

not tighten bolts. Center the flange by using tool SVO 2439 (SVO 2817 for the B30). Rotate the tool while tightening the bolts and adjusting the position of the flange. After tightening, the tool should rotate easily if the flange is properly positioned.

Guide Bearing Inspection

The guide bearing for the clutch shaft should be replaced if worn. To inspect, remove lock ring and washer and pull bearing with SVO 4090. Tool SVO 1426 is used to install new bearing after packing with heat-resistant bearing grease.

Oil Pump Inspection

The oil pump should be checked for worn or damaged bushings and for gear clearance. Play in the shafts should measure .0008–.004″ (.02–.10 mm), and gear lash clearance .006–1.014″ (.15–.35 mm). Check relief valve spring to see that it is not worn or collapsed. The relief valve plunger is removed by using tool SVO 2079.

Measuring oil pump gear backlash.

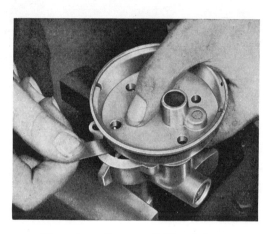

Measuring oil pump shaft end-play.

Torque Specifications

Engine	Cyl. Head (Ft. Lb.)	Main Bear. Bolts (Ft. Lb.)	Rod Bear. Bolts (Ft. Lb.)	Crank-shaft Pulley Bolt (Ft. Lb.)	Flywheel to Crank-shaft Bolts (Ft. Lb.)	Camshaft Nut (Ft. Lb.)	Gen. or Alt. Bolt (Ft. Lb.)	Oil Cooler Nut (Ft. Lb.)	Oil Filter Nipple (Ft. Lb.)	Oil Pan Bolts (Ft. Lb.)
B-18	61-69	87-94	38-42	51-58	33-40	94-108	25-29	22-25	33-40	6-8
B-20	61-69	87-94	38-42	51-58	33-40	94-108	45-75		33-40	6-8
B-30	61-69	87-94	38-42	51-58	36-40	94-108			33-40	7.3-8.7

Fuel System

Many fuel system problems result from accumulated deposits, restricted tank ventilation, leaky lines and connections, and worn moving parts. These troubles can be eliminated efficiently if they are identified *before* assembly. See Chapter 2, *Hard Starting, Poor Performance—Tuning*, for detailed procedures in locating poor-performance problems.

Pressure Test

Fuel pressure is determined by diaphragm spring tension in the fuel pump.

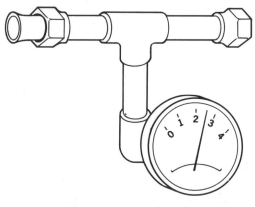

Measuring fuel pump pressure.

A weak spring causes low fuel pressure. Extreme spring tension creates fuel pressures that are too high. Pressures for normal engines range between 1.7 to 2.5 psi. To check pressure, insert a "T" in the line at the pump outlet to the carburetors and connect a pressure gauge to it. A pressure drop after the engine has stopped means a leaky pump valve or carburetor float valve.

Reconditioning Fuel Pump

There are four types of diaphragm fuel pumps used in the Volvo. Type I is an AC-UG, Type II is a Pierburg APG, Type III is an AC-YD, and Type IV is a Pierburg PV 3025. The strainer is removed from Type I by releasing the clip and removing the glass. On Types II and III the cover is removed. On Type IV, the strainer is part of the plug on the side of the pump. Remove the strainer and blow air through it. Replace with new strainer and gasket, if necessary, when reassembling.

Carefully remove fuel lines and remove pump from engine housing. Procedures for disassembling the three types of pumps differ slightly and are treated separately:

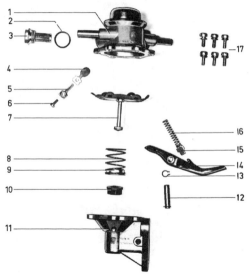

1. Upper housing
2. Sealing washer
3. Plug and strainer
4. Inlet valve
5. Stop arm
6. Screw
7. Diaphragm
8. Spring
9. Spring guide
10. Rubber seal
11. Lower pump housing
12. Lever pin
13. Snap-ring
14. Lever
15. Spring retainer
16. Return spring
17. Housing bolts

Fuel pump, Type IV, disassembled.

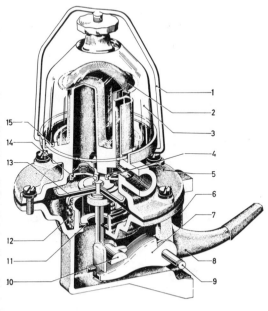

1. Retaining clamp
2. Strainer
3. Sludge trap
4. Inlet valve
5. Upper pump housing
6. Lower pump housing
7. Link arm
8. Rocker arm
9. Shaft
10. Stop
11. Seal
12. Spring
13. Diaphragm
14. Outlet valve
15. Gasket

Type I fuel pump.

Type I

Separate the upper and lower parts of the pump. Remove the diaphragm by pressing it down and turning it a quarter turn. Remove rocker arm shaft lock-ring and press out shaft. Remove rocker arm, spring, link arm and washers.

Replace the valves (in an earlier design) by removing the screws for the retainer. Remove the old valves and clean recesses. Place new valves and new seats in position and install retainer.

Replace the valves (in a later design) by removing the old valves with a screwdriver and cleaning the valve recesses. Place new seals and valves in position using a sleeve. Then peen over the metal around each valve at four places with a special punch.

Assemble in reverse order, installing new diaphragm by pressing down rod in position and turning it a quarter turn. When installing make sure rocker arm lever is in correct position above its cam.

Types II and IV

Scratch line-up marks on the upper and lower parts. Separate the parts. Remove rocker arm pin lockring and press out pin. Pull out rocker arm and return-spring. Remove diaphragm with spring, guide and rubber seal. The spring can be removed after the rubber seal has been pulled up over the nylon washer. Remove screw on the underside of the upper part, remove the stop arm and the spring valve. The inlet valve cannot be removed.

The inlet valve on the Type II and the outlet valve on the Type IV cannot be removed. Start assembling the Type II by inserting the leaf spring and stop arm. On the Type IV fit the inlet valve and stop arm. Tighten screw just enough for leaf spring to contact pump housing properly. Install spring and guide, and pull on rubber seal with flange inward, facing guide. Install diaphragm unit in lower part of pump. Press downward so that the rubber seal comes into correct position. Press down diaphragm, push in rocker arm and make sure that it positions correctly in relation to the diaphragm rod. Install rocker arm pin, lock-ring, spring retainer and return-spring.

Assemble upper and lower parts in accordance with lineup marks and bolt to housing. Make sure rocker arm is in correct position above cam.

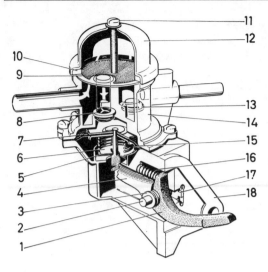

1. Rocker arm
2. Pin
3. Washer
4. Lever
5. Rubber seal
6. Washer
7. Diaphragm
8. Inlet valve
9. Strainer
10. Gasket
11. Screw with washer
12. Cover
13. Outlet valve
14. Upper pump housing
15. Diaphragm spring
16. Return spring
17. Rider
18. Lower pump housing

Type III fuel pump.

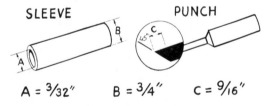

SLEEVE   PUNCH

A = 3/32″   B = 3/4″   C = 9/16″

Tools for inserting fuel pump valves.

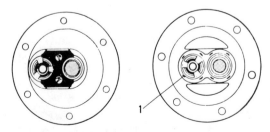

Installing valves in fuel pump. Earlier design at left, later design at right. 1=Peen.

Type III

Remove cover. Make scratch lineup marks on upper and lower parts, and separate the parts. Remove diaphragm by turning it one quarter turn. Remove diaphragm spring by turning washer so that hole coincides with wide end of diaphragm rod. With a grinding rod, remove peening for the rocker arm pin rider and remove rocker arm with pin and lever. Pull out rocker arm pin. Check parts for wear.

Assemble the pump by assembling the link arm, rocker arm with washers and the rocker arm pin. Insert linkage system with return spring into the housing. Install and lock riders in housing by peening.

SU Carburetor Principles

The dual SU carburetors used on the B14A, B16B, B18B and B20 engines are synchronized, variable venturi types. The front carb feeds the first and second cylinders and the rear carb feeds the third and fourth. Except for the vacuum nipple and float chamber, operation of the two carbs is identical. A needle valve of specially hardened steel gives dependable service over long periods of time.

Construction is extremely simple. Idling, acceleration, deceleration and constant high output are accomplished using a single nozzle. None of the fuel systems of conventional venturi carburetors is required.

Venturi area changes automatically with engine air intake. Thus, the speed of the air flowing through the venturi is nearly constant under all engine operating conditions.

Venturi Control

Venturi opening is varied by a suction piston sliding up and down within a suction chamber. The piston is moved by the differences in pressures above and below the piston. Venturi vacuum pressure is applied to the head of the piston through the suction port, and atmospheric pressure in the air filter is introduced through the air intake port below the piston. Thus,

6. Jet metering needle
7. Needle set screw
8. Piston spring
15. Jet sleeve set screw
18. Idling adjusting nut
22. Idling adjusting
     spring

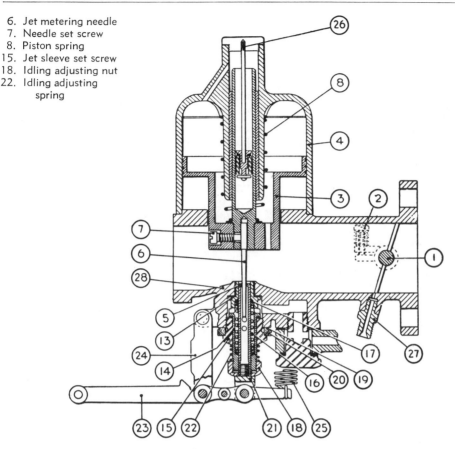

S.U. carburetor (float chamber not shown).

when the throttle plate is opened, the increased flow of engine intake air increases the vacuum pressure of the venturi, lifting the piston and enlarging the venturi. When the throttle plate is closed, reduced engine intake air decreases the vacuum pressure of the venturi and the piston lowers, constricting the venturi opening. Balance is maintained between the pressures acting upon the piston and the force of a piston spring, both being properly calibrated for optimum engine operation. In addition, an oil damper prevents the piston from opening too suddenly during acceleration.

Fuel Control

The suction piston also controls the up and down movement of a tapered metering needle in a fuel jet below the piston, automatically changing the amount of fuel

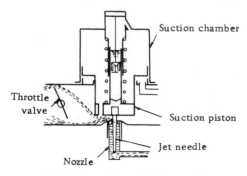

Venturi opening at idling speed.

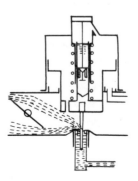

Venturi opening at medium low speed.

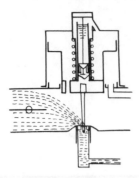

Venturi opening at high speed.

sucked into the throat of the carburetor by vacuum in the venturi.

Clearance between the metering needle and the jet is increased manually by pulling the choke knob, which through linkage, draws the jet down and increases the amount of fuel fed to the system. The throttle plate is automatically set by the connecting linkage to the proper opening for starting.

Float Chamber

The float chamber is nearly identical to that of conventional carburetors. Fuel is fed from the lower part of the float chamber, through a flexible hose to the jet at the bottom of the carburetor.

SU Carburetor Disassembly

The SU carburetors can be disassembled after removal from the vehicle as described in Chapter Two. However, the carburetors must be handled very carefully since venturi and fuel system are made of special high precision parts.

Suction Piston and Chamber

Remove the four set screws and take off the suction chamber. Remove suction spring, nylon packing and suction piston from chamber after placing components on a flat working surface so that the inside of the chamber and the sliding part of the piston are not damaged. Use extreme care not to bend the tapered fuel jet needle on the bottom of the piston.

Do not remove metering needle from suction piston unless absolutely necessary.

When it must be removed, first loosen the needle set screw. Then with pliers, grasp the needle at its shoulder near the piston and remove by slowly turning and pulling.

Performance will be adversely affected unless the metering needle is installed correctly in the piston. To do so, carefully push needle into piston until the shoulder is flush with the bottom. Wash and air-dry parts, then apply a few drops of light oil to the piston rod and reassemble. Do not apply oil to the large end of the piston or to the inside of the suction chamber.

Fuel Jet

The fuel jet is easily removed. However, the jet itself is a precision component and should not be disassembled unless absolutely necessary because reassembly is very difficult.

To remove jet, remove small (.1575 in. dia.) screw and then the connecting plate from the jet head. This is done easier by pulling lightly on the choke lever. Next, loosen clip and remove fuel line. The fuel jet can then be removed. When the jet is removed the metering needle will stay

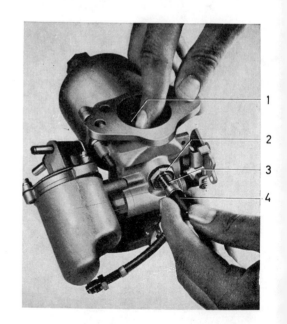

1. Lower part of vac-   3. Jet sleeve
   uum piston   4. Jet
2. Locknut

Centering the jet on S. U. carburetors.

inside. Be careful not to damage either. Next, remove the idling adjusting nut and spring. The fuel jet sleeve is removed by removing the sleeve set screw. Clean and air-dry the jet.

Reassemble in reverse order, removing the oil cap nut to assist in centering piston in suction chamber. Set piston to its fully closed position and insert fuel jet until it contacts the jet sleeve. Then move jet sleeve slightly so that it is at right angles to the center axis, and position the jet sleeve so that the jet does not contact needle.

Raise suction piston with the finger, and lower it slowly. Piston should drop smoothly until stop-pin drops on venturi making a light striking sound. Tighten jet sleeve set screw at this position. Now remove jet and install idle adjusting spring and nut on jet sleeve and re-insert jet. Connect fuel line to jet nipple. Next, pull choke lever slightly, hold connecting plate with sleeve and .1575 in.-diameter washer and tighten it on jet head with the .1575 in.-diameter screw. In so doing, move choke lever slightly and attach sleeve firmly to connecting plate opening. Upon completion of assembly, again check that suction piston drops smoothly.

SU Carburetor Adjustment
(See Chapter Two)

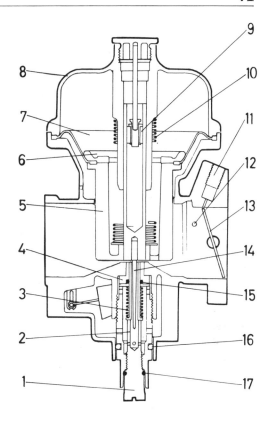

1. Orifice adjusting screw
2. Jet holder
3. Spring
4. Guide
5. Air valve
6. Washer
7. Diaphragm
8. Suction chamber
9. Damper piston
10. Spring
11. Vacuum connection
12. Cold start fuel channel
13. Throttle flap
14. Metering needle
15.-17. O-rings

Zenish-Stromberg 175-CD-2S Carburetor.

Zenith-Stromberg 175-CD-2S/2SE Carburetor

The Zenith-Stromberg Type 175-CD-2S/2SE carburetor used on some B18, most B20B and all B30A engines, is a single jet horizontal carburetor. Fuel flow through the jet is controlled by a tapered metering needle attached to the air valve and diaphragm which is operated by the carburetor vacuum. The jet is mounted at the bottom of the carburetor and is adjustable.

When the engine is idling, vacuum in the intake manifold and suction chamber of the carburetor is low and the metering needle is inserted further into the jet, allowing only a small quantity of fuel to enter the engine. With the opening of the throttle plate for higher speeds, pressure on one side of the valve and vacuum on the other causes the valve to lift and pull the metering needle out of the jet, increasing fuel flow. A variable choke area between the bridge and valve maintains an approximately constant air velocity and pressure across the jet, assuring good fuel atomization at all speeds.

At the moment of acceleration, a temporary, richer mixture is provided by a damper that operates in oil. When the throttle is suddenly opened, the vacuum in the suction chamber lifts the valve and forces the damper piston against its seat preventing oil from flowing from the upper side to the lower side of the piston. This momentarily retards the movement of the valve, causing a super vacuum above the jet and making the fuel-air mixture richer.

175-CD-2S/2SE Disassembly

Remove carburetor from vehicle after disconnecting fuel line, throttle and choke controls, vacuum line to the distributor, and removing screws holding carburetor to intake manifold.

Scratch alignment marks (for reassembly) on the suction chamber and body. Remove suction chamber and spring. Remove screws and washer, with diaphragm and piston. Loosen screw and remove metering needle.

Remove float chamber. Carefully remove float shaft from the bridge and remove the float. Unscrew and remove jet holder, adjusting screw, jet spring, guide and washers. Remove fuel inlet needle and washer. Remove choke device. Wash and air-dry components. Use kerosene only for washing diaphragm.

Check diaphragm for damage. Replace if cracked or distorted. Check metering needle for wear. If bent or worn replace needle. Check contacting and sealing surfaces for damage. Check valve disc on choke device.

Assemble carburetor by placing diaphragm on air valve so that projection fits into recess in valve and guiding edge fits into slit. If diaphragm is too distorted to fit, replace it. Place washer over diaphragm so that screw holes line without turning washer, and washer groove mates with guide edge of diaphragm. Tighten screws.

Fit metering needle with cylindrical section of needle against valve. Install valve and diaphragm into carb body, fitting tag into recess. Install suction chamber observing alignment marks. The slit and guiding edge should fit easily. Insert screws.

Insert adjusting screw together with the new O-ring into jet holder, and install new O-ring on the jet holder. Install the spring, brass washer, guide, new O-ring and washer on the jet, and install the entire assembly together with the jet holder and adjusting screw into the carb body. Screw

in the jet holder by hand but do not tighten it. Screw in the adjusting screw until the upper part of the jet is against the air valve when the valve is at its lowest position. Position the carburetor with the flange on the throttle plate side down and allow the air valve to fall. The needle will then enter the fuel jet orifice and automatically centralize the jet. Tighten jet assembly slowly, frequently checking to see that the needle remains free in the orifice. Raise the air valve and allow it to fall freely. The piston should then stop firmly on the bridge. After the jet is tight, if a clear striking sound is not heard when the piston is lifted and allowed to fall, repeat the centering procedure.

Install the float and shaft with the flat side of the float facing away from the carb body. Check the float level. The highest point on the float (front) should be ⅝" above the face of the body and the rear edge ¼" above. Float level can be changed by carefully bending the tab which connects to the end of the needle. Do not bend the float arm.

Install a new gasket on the float chamber and install float chamber, inserting all screws just a few turns. Then move float chamber down to the contact surface of upper section and tighten screws. Install choke device.

175-CD-2S/2SE Adjustment

(See Chapter Two)

Zenith 34VN/36VN Carburetors

Single Zenith Type 34VN or 36VN downdraft carburetors are used on the Volvo B16A, B16D and some of the B18A engines. Fuel is fed through fixed jets and mixed with air fed into the venturi.

A manually operated choke control operates a cam-shaped lever to close the choke plate causing a high vacuum and consequently a larger supply of fuel. When the engine has started and the vacuum increases, the choke plate can open itself to some extent since the closing force is from a spring on the choke shaft. Pushing in the choke knob forces the choke plate to open fully.

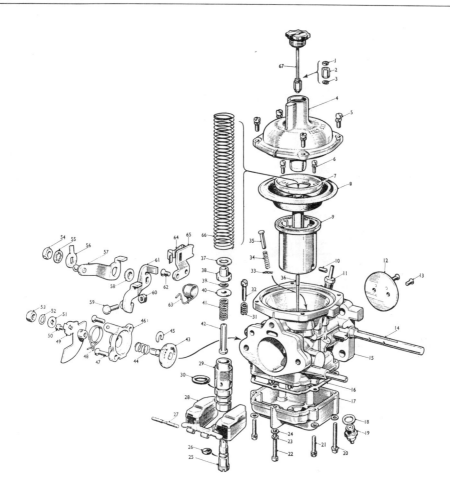

1. Washer	23. Spring washer (6 off)	47. Screw for do. (2 off)
2. Bush	24. Washer (6 off)	Shakeproof washer (2 off)
3. Retaining ring	25. Adjusting screw (incl. item 26)	(not shown)
4. Cover	26. "O" ring for do.	48. Return spring
5. Screw and spring washer	27. Float pin	49. Cam lever assy.
(4 off)	28. Float assembly	50. Clamping screw
6. Screw and spring washer	29. Bush retaining screw (incl.	51. Spacing washer
(4 off)	item 30)	52. Shakeproof washer
7. Retaining ring	30. "O" ring for do	53. Nut
8. Diaphragm	31. Spring	54. Nut for throttle spindle
9. Air valve and shaft	32. Throttle stop screw	55. Shakeproof washer
Air valve assy. (incl. items	33. Clip	56. Tab washer
6, 7, 8 and 9)	34. Spring	57. Throttle lever
10. Locking screw	35. Lifting pin	58. Bush
11. Ignition adapter	36. Metering needle	59. Fast-idle screw
12. Throttle	37. Washer for bush	60. Locknut for do.
13. Screw (2 off)	38. Bush for jet	61. Throttle stop and fast-idle
14. Throttle spindle	39. "O" ring	lever
15. Main body	40. Washer for "O" ring	62. Screw for control bracket
16. Gasket	41. Spring for jet	63. Throttle return spring
17. Floatchamber	42. Jet	64. Clip for control bracket
18. Washer	43. Starter spindle assy.	65. Starter control bracket
19. Needle valve	44. Starter spring	66. Air valve return spring
20. See item 22	45. "C" washer	67. Damper assy. (incl. items 1,
21. Screw (short) (2 off)	46. Starter cover	2 and 3)
22. Screw (long) (4 off)		

Stromberg 175 CD-2S Carburetor, Exploded View.

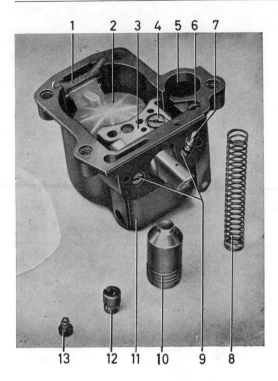

1 2 3 4 5 6 7

13 12 11 10 9 8

1. Lock spring	7. Acceleration jet
(Marked TOP)	8. Plunger spring
2. Float	9. Screws attaching
3. Emulsion block	emulsion block
4. Idling air jet	10. Plunger
5. Acceleration pump	11. Float chamber
barrel	12. Inlet valve
6. Outlet valve	13. Stop screw

Zenith 34VN/36VN carburetor float chamber.

One of the cams on the choke lever also actuates the throttle plate through the rapid idling screw linkage. This causes the throttle plate to open at the same time the choke plate closes. The degree to which the throttle plate opens relative to the closing of the choke plate is determined by the setting of the rapid idling screw.

While the engine is idling, the throttle plate is almost completely closed, its position determined by an idling stop screw. Fuel is sucked up by high vacuum from a passage above the main jet, through a hole and the idling jet, into a passage that terminates in the throat of the carburetor. Fuel-air mixture is controlled by an idle adjusting screw.

Although a large part of the fuel fed to the engine at high speeds passes through the main jet, this jet alone cannot supply a well balanced amount of fuel under all conditions. Therefore, a third jet, known as a compensation jet, works in conjunction with the main jet to supply additional fuel. The amount of air added is controlled by an economizer valve, the air-fuel mixture ratio being higher when the vacuum in the carburetor venturi is large. When the throttle is opened quickly, the fuel-air mixture has a tendency to be too lean. To overcome this, fuel is sprayed into the carburetor venturi by an acceleration pump that is actuated by spring loaded linkage connected to the throttle controls.

34VN/36VN Disassembly

To clean the carburetor, it is usually sufficient to remove the float chamber, and float, remove the idling jet and the air jet located above it, remove the acceleration pump plunger and the idle fuel screw on the housing. Remove the needle valve. Wash all parts in kerosene or alcohol and air-dry. Blow compressed air through all channels and jets, including hole for idle fuel screw. Hold jets up to light to check for cleanliness.

To disassemble, remove float chamber. Remove float lever and float. Remove emulsion block and remove all jets from block. Remove acceleration pump plunger, spring inlet valve, outlet valve and acceleration jet. Remove float valve and economizer valve. Unscrew idle fuel jet. Blow all parts dry with compressed air after cleaning. Do not use wire to clean jets.

Reassemble in reverse order, making sure that all gaskets and parts are in good condition. Observe TOP markings on float and float lever. Press float chamber upwards and inwards against carb body and then tighten screws. Check that the emulsion block is in contact with the stay across the venturi. If not, loosen the screw, adjust the position and tighten screw.

34VN/36VN Adjustment

(See Chapter Two)

Carburetor Specifications

Engine Model	Carburetor(s)	Air Intake Dia. In.	Venturi Desig.	Fuel Control Jet Dia. (in.)	Desig.	Main Jet (Standard) Dia. (in.)	Desig.	Compensating Dia. (mm)	Jet Desig.	Needle Type	Idle Fuel Jet Dia. (mm)	Desig.	Idle Air Jet Dia. (mm)	Desig.	Accel. Dia. (mm)	Jet Desig.	Float Valve (dim.)	Float Valve Washer (thickness mm)	Fuel Level (Below Float Bowl Top)	Idling Speed RPM — Warm Engine
B-14A	SU H2(2)	1.5		.09						CZ										
B-16A	Zenith 34VN		27			.97		.97	97		.50		.50		.40	.40		1	18mm	400–600
B-16B	SU H4(2)	1.5			AUC 2112					GT*										500–700
B-18A	Zenith 36VN		30			117			115		70		70		40		1.75	1		500–700
B-18B, D	SU H6(2)	1.75								KA										500–700
B-18D	Zenith-Stromberg 175CD-2S																			
B-20A	Zenith-Stromberg 175CD-2SE	1.63																		700
B-20B	SU HS6	1.63																		700
	Zenith-Stromberg 175CD-2SE	1.63																		700
B-30A	Zenith-Stromberg 175CD-2SE	1.63																		750
	SU HS6																			750

*GW when using intake silencer air cleaner.

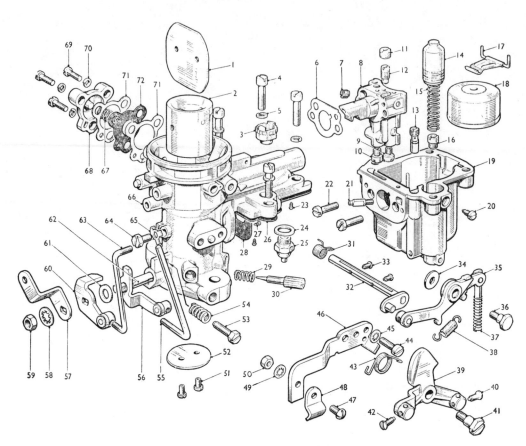

Zenith 34 VN Carburetor, Exploded View.

1. Strangler flap
2. Choke tube
3. Pump stop
4. Screw and spring washer fixing bowl to barrel (4 off)
5. See item 4
6. Gasket for emulsion block
7. Not used
8. Emulsion block
9. Compensating jet
10. Main jet
11. Plug over slow-running jet
12. Slow-running jet
13. Pump discharge valve
14. Pump piston
15. Spring for do.
16. Pump check valve
17. Float arm and pivot
18. Float
19. Carburetor bowl
20. Stop screw for pump piston
21. Pump jet
22. Screw fixing emulsion block (2 off)
23. Drive screw fixing item 26 (4 off)
24. Washer for needle and seating
25. Needle and seating
26. Gasket (bowl to barrel) (horizontal face)
27. Drive screw fixing item 28 (2 off) (see item 23)

28. Gasket (bowl to barrel) (vertical face)
29. Spring for volume control screw
30. Volume control screw
31. Automaticity spring
32. Strangler spindle and lever assembly
33. Screw fixing strangler flap (2 off)
    Washer for strangler spindle (not shown)
34. Washer for pivot screw
35. Pump lever and rod assembly (includes item 38)
36. Pivot screw for pump lever
37. Spring for pump rod
    Sealing washer for pump rod (not shown)
38. Follow-up spring
39. Strangler control lever
40. Screw for strangler swivel
41. Pivot screw for strangler control lever
42. Screw for interconnection swivel
43. Spring for strangler control lever
44. Screw fixing strangler control bracket
45. Shakeproof washer

46. Strangler control bracket (includes items 47, 48, 49 and 50)
47. Screw fixing clip
48. Clip
49. Shakeproof washer
50. Nut
51. Screw fixing throtle (2 off)
52. Throttle
53. Throttle stop screw
54. Spring for do.
55. Interconnection rod
56. Floating lever
57. Throttle lever
58. Shakeproof washer
59. Nut
60. Throttle stop
61. Washer
62. Throttle spindle
63. Pump link
64. Screw fixing choke tube
65. Tab washer for do.
66. Carburetor barrel assembly
67. Economy spring
68. Economy valve cover
69. Screw fixing do. (3 off)
70. Spring washer for screw (3 off)
71. Gasket for economy diaphragm (2 off)
72. Economy diaphragm

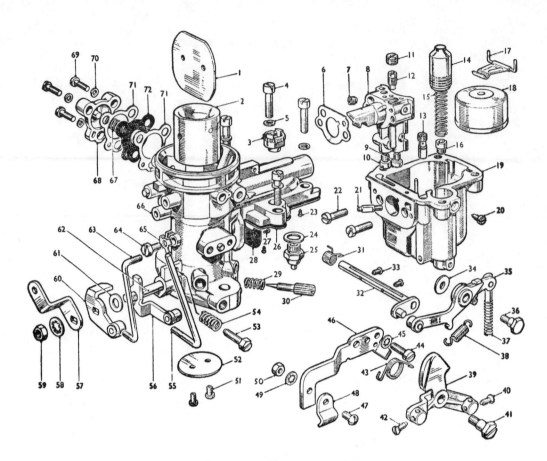

Zenith 36 VN Carburetor, Exploded View.

1. Strangler flap
2. Choke tube
3. Pump stop
4. Screw and spring washer fixing bowl to barrel (4 off)
5. See item 4
6. Gasket for emulsion block
7. Ventilation screw
8. Emulsion block
9. Compensating jet
10. Main jet
11. Plug over slow-running jet
12. Slow-running jet
13. Pump discharge valve
14. Pump piston
15. Spring for pump piston
16. Pump check valve
17. Float arm and pivot (not used)
18. Float and arm
    Float arm pivot (not shown)
    Float arm retainer (not shown)
19. Carburetor bowl
20. Stop screw for pump piston
21. Pump jet
22. Screw fixing emulsion block (2 off)
23. Drive screw fixing item 26 (4 off)
24. Washer for needle valve
25. Needle valve
26. Gasket (bowl to barrel) (horizontal face)
27. Drive screw fixing item 28 (2 off) (see item 23)
28. Gasket (bowl to barrel) (vertical face)

29. Spring for volume control screw
30. Volume control screw
31. Automaticity spring
32. Strangler spindle and lever assembly
    Washer for strangler spindle (not shown)
33. Screw fixing strangler flap (2 off)
34. Washer for pivot screw
35. Pump lever and rod assembly (includes item 38)
36. Pivot screw for pump lever
    Sealing washer for pump rod (not shown)
37. Spring for pump rod
38. Follow-up spring
39. Strangler control lever
40. Screw for strangler swivel
41. Pivot screw for strangler control lever
42. Not used
43. Spring for strangler control lever
44. Screw fixing strangler control bracket
45. Shakeproof washer
46. Strangler control bracket (assembled with items 47, 48, 49 and 50)
47. Screw fixing clip
48. Clip
49. Shakeproof washer
50. Nut
51. Screw fixing throttle (2 off)
52. Throttle
53. Throttle stop screw

54. Spring for throttle stop screw
55-56. Not used
57. Throttle lever
    Spring washer (not shown)
58. Shakeproof washer
59. Nut
60. Throttle stop
61. Washer
62. Throttle spindle
63. Pump link
64. Screw fixing choke tube
65. Tab washer for screw
66. Carburetor body assembly
67. Economy springs
68. Economy valve cover
69. Screw fixing valve cover (3 off)
70. Spring washer for screw (3 off)
71. Gasket for economy diaphragm (2 off)
72. Economy diaphragm
    Carburetor assembled complete

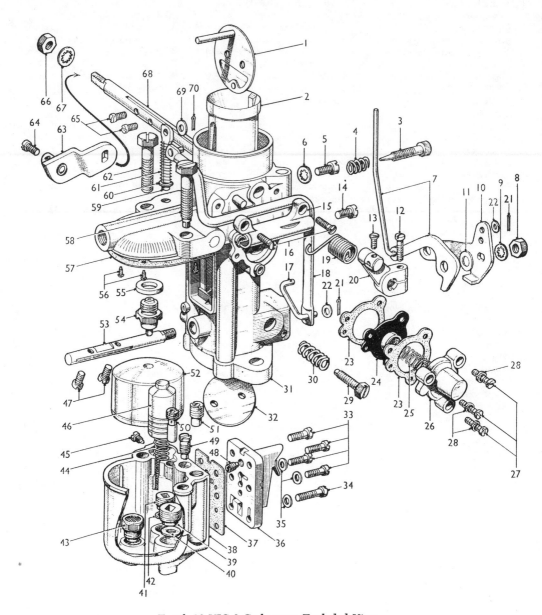

Zenith 30 VIG-9 Carburetor, Exploded View.

1. Strangler flap
2. Choke tube
3. Air regulating screw
4. Spring for do.
5. Screw for strangler bracket
6. Shakeproof washer
7. Floating lever and interconnection link assembly
8. Nut for throttle spindle
9. Shakeproof washer for do.
10. Throttle lever
11. Washer for throttle spindle
12. Screw clamping strangler lever
13. Screw for strangler lever swivel
14. Choke screw
    Shakeproof washer for do. (not shown)
15. Bearing plate for pump control
16. Screw fixing do. (2 off)
17. Pump control link
18. Pump control lever
    Pump control lever (assembled with items 17, 21, 22, 59, 69 and 70)
19. Spring for strangler spindle
20. Strangler lever
21. Split pin for pump link (2 off)
22. Washer for pump link (2 off)
23. Gasket for economy diaphragm (2 off)
24. Economy diaphragm
25. Economy spring
26. Economy valve cover
27. Screw fixing do. (3 off)
28. Spring washer for screw (3 off)

29. Throttle stop screw
30. Spring for do.
31. Carburetor barrel (assembled with items 3, 4, 7, 8, 9, 10, 11, 23, 24, 25, 26, 27, 28, 32, 47, 53, 56 and 57)
32. Throttle
33. Screw fixing emulsion block (short) (4 off)
34. Screw fixing emulsion block (long)
35. Washer for lower emulsion block screw (3 off)
36. Emulsion block
37. Gasket for do.
38. Carburetor bowl
39. Compensating jet
40. Washer for do.
41. Main jet
42. Washer for do.
43. Pump check valve
44. Spring for pump piston
45. Stop screw for do.
46. Pump piston
47. Screw fixing throttle (2 off)
48. Pump jet
49. Slow-running jet
50. Ball valve for pump circuit
51. Screw over capacity well
52. Float
53. Throttle spindle
54. Needle seating
55. Washer for do.
56. Drive screw fixing gasket (4 off)
57. Gasket (bowl to barrel)
58. Screw fixing bowl (jet key type)

59. Pump rod
60. Washer for do.
61. Spring for pump rod
62. Screw fixing bowl (plain type)
63. Interconnection lever (assembled with item 64)
64. Screw for swivel
65. Screw fixing strangler flap (2 off)
66. Nut fixing interconnection lever
67. Shakeproof washer for do.
68. Strangler spindle
69. Washer for pump rod
70. Split pin for pump rod pivot
    Carburetor assembled complete

Volvos equipped with B14 and B16 engines employ six-volt electrical systems, and Volvos with B18, B20 and B30 engines employ 12-volt systems. Each consists of the battery, starter, generator or alternator, regulator, ignition, lighting, signaling and instrumentation components.

Component Description, Removal and Repair

Battery

The battery in B18 and B20 engines is mounted on a shelf to the left of the radiator; on the B30 it is to the right of the radiator. It is a 12-volt, lead-acid battery with a capacity of 60 ampere hours and the negative terminal is grounded. The battery for the B14 and B16 engines is mounted on a shelf on the front bulkhead. It is a 6-volt, lead-acid battery with a capacity of 85 ampere hours and the negative terminal is grounded.

BATTERY REPLACEMENT

Loosen the bolts of the battery cable clamps. Spread the clamps with a screw-driver and then use a clamp puller if necessary, to remove the clamp. Pulling on the clamp itself may damage the battery. Note polarity of battery connections.

Remove screws from battery clamp and remove battery from car. Clean battery with a brush and rinse with lukewarm water. Clean the battery shelf and cable clamps with a wire brush. Install new battery in proper position and install clamp and screws. Coat cable clamps and battery terminals with vaseline.

Starter

The starter is mounted on the left side of the flywheel housing. It consists of a 4-pole, series-wound motor. The motor is energized by a solenoid which also engages the gear of the starter clutch assembly with the flywheel ring gear.

The field frame carries the pole shoes and the field coils. The armature has a spline which carries the over-running clutch and gear assembly. The armature shaft is supported in two bushings which are permanently packed with lubricant.

As the starter is energized, the shift lever moves against the spring and by means of the guide ring sends the gear

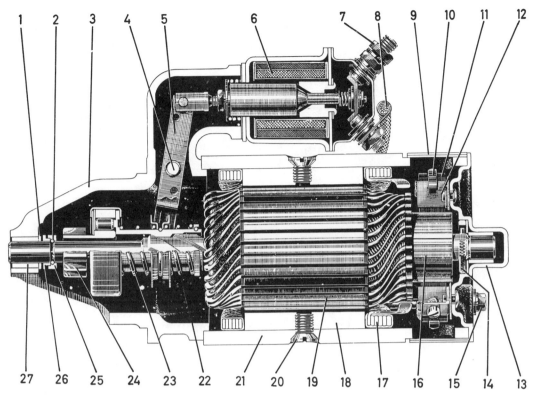

1. Adjusting washer
5. Clutch lever
6. Solenoid switch
7. Battery lead terminal
8. Starter motor terminal
11. Brush assembly

14. Armature brake
16. Commutator
17. Field winding
18. Pole shoe
19. Armature
20. Pole screw

23. Clutch spring
24. Clutch gear
25. Stop washer
26. Stop washer
27. Bushing

Starter and solenoid components.

into mesh with the flywheel. After the gear meshes, the solenoid contact disc closes the circuit and the engine is cranked. When the engine starts, the increased speed of the flywheel causes the gear to over-run the clutch and armature. The gear continues in full mesh until the starter current is interrupted. Then the shift lever spring returns the gear to its neutral position.

STARTER REPLACEMENT

If troubleshooting tests (See Chapter Two) indicate that the starter is defective, the unit can be removed from the vehicle as follows.

Remove the battery ground cable so that the cables connected to the starter are not "hot". Disconnect leads from starter, noting connections. Remove bolts holding starter to flywheel housing and lift starter off. Install new starter in reverse order from above. Tighten bolts evenly, but not too tightly. Connect leads to starter terminals. Connect battery ground cable.

STARTER DISASSEMBLY

The starter may be disassembled for overhaul or repair as follows after removal from the vehicle:

Remove the cover protecting the brushes and commutator. Remove brush screws, lift springs and remove brushes. Mark position of front and rear end frames in relation to the housing and remove through-bolts that hold these frames to the housing. Disconnect lead between the control solenoid and housing and lift off the rear end frame with armature brake together

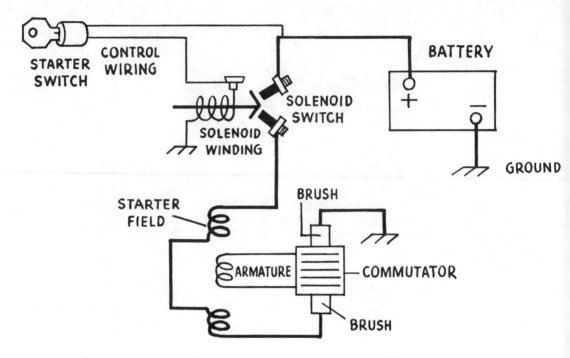

Schematic diagram of starter electrical circuit.

1. Battery lead terminal
2. Starter switch terminal
3. Starter field terminal

Rear of starter and end cover plate that must be removed for starter disassembly.

with the housing. Remove pivot screw from solenoid engaging fork, and lift out armature and clutch assembly from housing. Remove the stop washers from the armature shaft. Three washers are removed by pulling straight off shaft. Tap the thick washer further onto the shaft about ¼" and remove the lock ring. Then remove the thick washer from the shaft.

Remove armature brake from rear end frame. Blow dirt and dust from housing, field winding and armature. Wipe clean but do not use solvents that may attack the insulation of the windings.

STARTER COMPONENT CHECKS

Examine the armature for damage such as bent or worn shaft, scored commutator or damaged windings. A defective shaft or damaged windings require armature replacement. A scored or unevenly worn armature can be turned using a special chuck.

Check the armature for electrical shorts by placing it in a growler machine and holding a thin piece of steel such as a hacksaw blade an inch or so from the armature. If the blade vibrates in any position when the armature is rotated in the growler, there is a short between frame and windings, between windings, or between commutator and frame. Locate short by checking with a low wattage lamp and test prods. A shorted armature usually must be rewound.

Examine the housing and check the field windings for damage to armature. Using test prods and the low wattage lamp, check the field winding by placing one test prod on the housing and one on the field lead. If the lamp lights, the field may be damaged, or the lead-through may be shorted at the housing. Remove lead-through and test again. If short continues, field must be replaced. Check end head containing brush holders and test the two normally insulated holders for shorts to the end head. If brush holders are shorted replace end head assembly.

STARTER ASSEMBLY

Install armature brake in rear end frame and install electrical lead between positive brushes. Install clutch gear on armature shaft, slide on washers and secure locking ring. Lubricate armature shaft and brake with silicone grease.

Assemble armature and gear housing and place engaging arm in its position around the gear. Install solenoid on gear housing and insert pivot screw. Lubricate gear and engaging arm with silicone grease. Lubricate shaft end.

Place housing over armature, lining up with the end frame according to markings made on casing before disassembly. Place rear end frame on armature shaft in correct position and assemble end frames and housing with through bolts. Tighten bolts. Install brushes. Turn armature, and check to see that it moves freely.

Install starter on vehicle by carrying out reverse procedure from removal. Tighten bolts evenly, but not too tightly. Install brush and commutator cover. Connect leads to starter terminals. Connect battery ground lead.

Generator

The generator, which is mounted on the right side of the engine and is driven by V-belt from the crankshaft, is a DC shunt-wound type. The current and voltage charging rates are controlled by a regulator mounted on the engine firewall.

The DC generator has a rotating armature with copper windings that intersect lines of magnetic force between magnetic field poles. At the start, the magnetic field is weak because it is only residual. However, as current flows from the armature windings, part of the flow is fed into and excites the magnetic field. Increasing speed intensifies the magnetic field and thereby increases the voltage from the windings. The magnetic field becomes saturated with energy and no further increase in armature speed will add to the output.

GENERATOR REPLACEMENT

If generator is found defective (See Chapter Two), replace as follows. Remove ground cable from negative terminal of battery. Disconnect leads from generator. Loosen V-belt tensioning bracket and remove belt. Remove two bolts holding generator to engine and lift off generator. Install new generator in reverse order of above, making sure connections are correct and that V-belt tension is adjusted as in Chapter One.

GENERATOR BENCH TEST

Clean outside of generator with rag moistened in kerosene. Remove brush

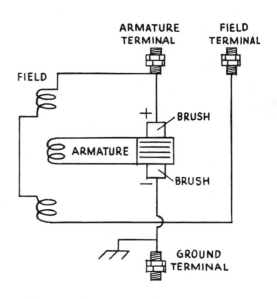

Schematic diagram of generator electrical circuit.

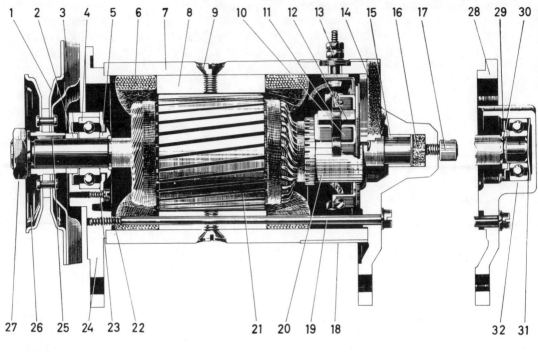

1. Belt pulley
2. Spacing ring
3. Oil seal washer
4. Ball bearing
5. Spacing ring
6. Filed winding
7. Stator
8. Pole shoe
9. Pole screw
10. Brush holder
11. Brush spring
12. Brush

13. Armature terminal
Gen. type AR6
14. End shield
15. Bushing
16. Lubricating felt
17. Lubricating cap
18. Protecting band
19. Through bolt
20. Commutator
21. Armature
22. Screw

23. Sealing washer
24. End head
25. Key
26. Spring washer
27. Nut
28. End shield
Gen. type AR7
29. Oil seal washer
30. Spacing ring
31. Spring ring
32. Ball bearing

DC generator components.

and commutator protective cover and check commutator for worn or scored surfaces. Inspect inside of generator housing around commutator for solder that may have been thrown from commutator as a result of overheating. If solder is present, generator is probably shorted and armature or field may require rewinding. If commutator and brushes are in good condition, make the following test.

Connect the generator field terminal to the generator ground terminal and to the negative terminal of a battery of the proper voltage (6V or 12V) for the generator under test. Connect the armature terminal of the generator in series with an ammeter to the positive terminal of the battery. The generator should then run as a motor at a low, even speed. If it does not run or runs very slowly, and the current is low, the trouble could be that brushes, not free in the holders, are making poor contact on the commutator, or a defective armature winding. If it does not run or runs slowly and the current is high, the trouble could be a broken or shorted field, a worn bushing, or too-high brush tension. Heavy sparking or excessive up and down movement of brushes means commutator is too far out-of-round, or brushes are damaged.

GENERATOR DISASSEMBLY

Generator may be dismantled for overhaul or repair as follows: remove brush and commutator cover. Disconnect brush

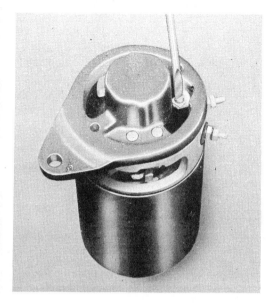

Removing generator connecting bar.

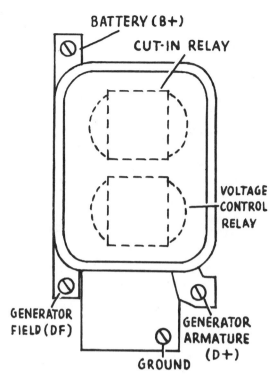

Regulator connections, 12-volt system.

leads and remove brushes. Remove terminal connecting bar and then remove through-bolts which hold end frames together.

Pull off rear end frame with brush holders, and lift armature out of housing. Place armature in a vise having soft jaws (avoid excessive tightening) and remove pulley nut, lock washer, pulley, fan, key, and drive end frame.

NOTE: *after removing armature from vise, tap threaded end of armature shaft with a soft hammer, if necessary, to remove drive end frame.* Remove bearing parts from drive end frame. Clean and inspect the ball bearings, replace worn parts, and pack assembly with high temperature grease. Wipe generator parts with clean cloth. Grease solvents might damage insulated windings. Reassemble using reverse sequence.

DC Regulator

The regulator is mounted on the right wheel housing and automatically controls the charging voltage and current that the generator supplies to the battery.

Since voltage produced by the generator is in direct ratio to the product of armature speed and exciting current in the magnetic field, a constant voltage output can be easily maintained by making compensating adjustments to the field current.

Armature speed is based on engine rpm and is therefore not independently controllable. The regulator maintains a constant voltage output by interrupting the field current.

The Bosch regulator used on the Volvo has a semi-conductor component, a variode, having a variable resistance under different voltage loads, ranging from high resistance at low voltages to extremely low resistance at high voltage levels. The variode lead picks up the voltage drop that resistance causes in the main current lead. The resistance of the main current lead determines the activation of the variode and should not be altered or replaced separately.

Regulator Adjustment-Cut-In Voltage

Connect an 0–20 DC voltmeter between the regulator terminal D+ and ground. Start engine and increase speed slowly, noting reading of voltmeter. The reading should first increase to about 6.1-6.4 (for 6V systems) and 12.1–12.8 (for 12V systems) then fall back to .1 or .2 volt when the cut-in relay is actuated, after which it should remain constant. Adjustment is car-

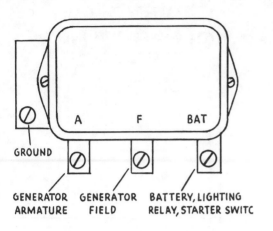

Regulator connections, 6-volt system.

GROUND

A   F   BAT

GENERATOR   GENERATOR   BATTERY, LIGHTING
ARMATURE   FIELD   RELAY, STARTER SWITC

ried out by decreasing the pressure of the spring on the cut-in relay. If it is too low, the adjustment is made by increasing the pressure on the spring.

REGULATOR ADJUSTMENT—CUT-OUT CURRENT

Connect an 0–50A ammeter in series with the battery (B+) connection to the regulator. Increase engine speed to obtain a reading. Then reduce speed gradually to idle, watching the ammeter reading go down to zero and slightly into the discharge region, when it should jump up suddenly to zero. At this point, the reverse current relay has cut out. If the reverse current (into discharge region) is less than 2 amps, the reverse current is too

low, and the tension of the contact spring on the cut-in relay should be lowered by bending the yoke of the cut-in contact. If the discharge reading is more than 7.5 amps, the bending of the contact spring must be increased until the cut-out current is within range.

REGULAR ADJUSTMENT—VOLTAGE CONTROL

Remove the wire from the B+ connection on the regulator. Connect a voltmeter between the B+ terminal on the regulator and ground, accelerate the engine gradually to increase the generator output. Watch the voltmeter reading increase and note the reading at which it stops increasing. This voltage for 6-volt systems should be 6.5–7.3, and for 12-volt systems, 13.9–14.9 for unloaded engines. Adjustment is made by bending the spring support to change spring pressure on the voltage control relay. Increasing spring pressure increases the voltage at which control takes place, decreasing spring pressure lowers the voltage. The engine should be thoroughly warmed before making this adjustment.

Alternator

The alternator is a three-phase, delta connected alternating unit. The rectifier, built into the slip ring end shield, consists of six silicon diodes. Also in the slip ring are the magnetizing diodes, which feed the field wiring via the voltage regulator. The alternator has a rotating field (rotor) and a stationary main wiring (stator).

1. Rectifier (positive diode plate)
2. Magnetizing rectifier
3. Brush holder
4. Slip ring end shield
5. Rectifier (negative diode)

6. Stator
7. Rotor
8. Drive end shield
9. Pulley with fan

Bosch alternator.

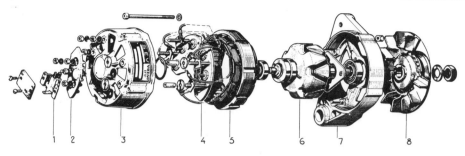

1. Brush holder
2. Insulation diode with holder
3. Slip ring end shield
4. Rectifier

5. Stator
6. Rotor
7. Drive end shield
8. Pulley with fan

Motorola alternator.

Since the alternator is self limiting as far as current is concerned (35 amps), a simple mechanical voltage regulator is used with only voltage control as its function.

ALTERNATOR REPLACEMENT

If the alternator is found defective (See Chapter Two), replace as follows.

Remove the negative lead from the battery. Disconnect the leads from the alternator. Loosen the tensioning bracket and the V-belt. Remove the bolt holding the alternator to the engine block, and remove the alternator.

Install new alternator in the reverse of above, making sure connections are correct and that the V-belt tension is adjusted as in Chapter One.

ALTERNATOR DISASSEMBLY

Remove the pulley and key. Remove the bolts holding the brush holder and take off the holder. Remove the nuts, washers and screws that hold the alternator together. Take off the drive end shield and rotor from the stator and slip off the ring end shield. Press the rotor out of the drive end shield. Remove the screws for the washer which holds the drive end shield bearing and press out the bearing.

On the Bosch, remove the positive diode plate and unsolder the stator connection to remove the stator. On the Motorola, remove the negative diode holder and the diode holders for the slip ring end shield.

Alternator Testing

Caution: do not use a 110 or 220 V DC or AC test lamp, or a high powered ohmmeter for any of the tests. Only a 12 V, 2-5 W test light should be used, and for testing the diodes only a battery-powered or other low powered ohmmeter should be used.

1. DF to field winding
2. 61/D+ from magnetizing rectifier
3. B+ to battery

Bosch alternator connections.

STATOR

Check stator isolation by connecting a 40 V alternating current between the body and each phase lead. If arcing or a noticeable odor is present, there is a short circuit. Another test is to use a 12 V, 2-5 W test lamp between the stator plates and a terminal on

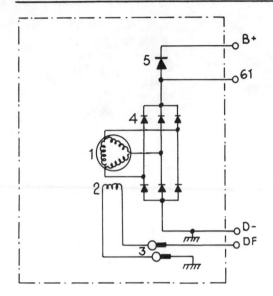

1. Stator
2. Rotor (field winding)
3. Slip rings and brush holder
4. Rectifier diode
5. Insulation diode

Motorola alternator inner circuit.

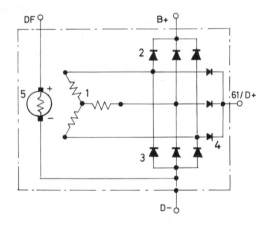

Inner wiring of Bosch alternator.

the stator. If the test lamp lights, the insulation is damaged and the stator must be replaced.

ROTOR

Check the rotor with a 40 V alternating current to the rotor frame and a slip ring. Arcing or a noticeable odor indicates a faulty rotor. Resistance between the slip

rings should be 4 ± 0.4 ohms on the Bosch alternator, and 5 ± 0.2 ohms for the Motorola alternator. Burned or damaged slip rings may be turned on the Bosch to a minimum of 1.3 in. (31.5 mm). Maximum out-of-roundness for the slip rings is 0.0012 in. (0.03 mm).

DIODES

Check the diodes with a diode tester or a battery-powered ohmmeter. When using an ohmmeter, resistance in one direction will be very high, and in the other direction will be very low.

To replace the diodes on the Bosch alternator, unsolder the faulty one and remove from the plate. Lubricate the replacement with silicon oil before inserting it. Paint a replaced positive diode with a chlorinated rubber enamel to prevent corrosion. If any of the magnetizing diodes are faulty, replace the entire plate with all the diodes.

To replace the diodes on the Motorola alternator, the entire diode holder must be replaced. If the isolation diode is faulty, the holder and the diode are replaced as a unit. The positive diode holder is marked with red ink and the negative diode holder is marked with black ink.

BRUSHES

Check the isolation of the brush holder with a 40 V alternating current as above. For the Bosch alternator minimum brush length is 0.32 in. (8 mm). For the Motorola alternator minimum brush length is 3/16 in. (5 mm). If less, replace the brushes.

ALTERNATOR ASSEMBLY

Fit the stator in the slip ring and shield, fit the diode holders and solder the stator leads to the connecting point. Grease the drive end bearing with light machine oil and fit the bearing and washer in the drive end bearing shield, then press the shield and the spacing ring onto the rotor. Lubricate the slip ring bearing and seat with a light layer of Moylkote or equivalent. Assemble alternator halves and lightly tighten the bolts. Fit the brush holder and pulley. Tighten the pulley nut to 29 ft. lbs.

AC Regulator

The regulator is mounted to the right of the radiator on the 140 series and on the right wheel well on the 164. It is a simple

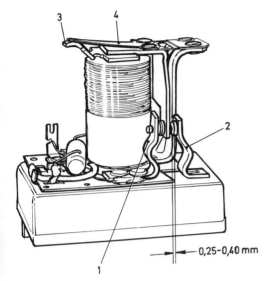

1. Regulator contact for lower control range (lower contact)
2. Regulator contact for upper control range (upper contact)
3. Stop lamp
4. Spring

Bosch AC voltage regulator.

mechanical device since the alternator is self-limiting.

Ignition System

A battery ignition system includes the ignition coil, contact-breaker, distributor, spark plugs, ignition switch, and a source of current. Current flows from the battery through the ignition switch to the induction coil. Through primary and secondary winding arrangements in the coil, high voltage is developed to fire the spark plugs. The distributor has two functions within the circuit. It has the breaker-point assembly which times the collapse of the magnetic field in the coil so that a pulse of high voltage (secondary circuit) is sent to the spark plugs. The second function of the distributor is the distribution of spark to the correct plug. The rotor and cap provide this distribution. The condenser, arranged in parallel with the breaker-point circuit, prevents arcing between the points after they have been separated. A precise instantaneous magnetic field collapse in the coil is thus possible.

DISTRIBUTOR REPLACEMENT

To remove the distributor for overhaul or replacement, remove the distributor cap, place No. 1 cylinder in the firing position (timing marks aligned), disconnect vacuum line and primary ignition wire, and remove bolt, clamp and distributor.

Replace paper gasket on distributor housing if necessary.

Install new distributor with vacuum advance unit pointing rearward and parallel with engine. Turn rotor to align mark on tip with breaker point hold-down screw so that shaft seats itself. If distributor was set in wrong, rotor will be 180° out of place. Set distributor into position and hand tighten bolt. The mark on the rotor should be nearly aligned with mark on distributor housing. Align marks on rotor tip and housing, set breaker

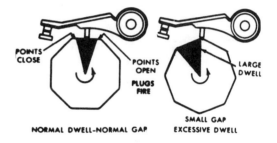

Distributor dwell angle.

point gap or dwell angle, and adjust ignition timing.

CONTACT-POINT ASSEMBLY

When installing points, lightly lubricate distributor cam with high temperature grease. CAUTION: *excessive lubricant will throw off into contact points.* Position support on breaker plate and install lock screw loosely for later adjustment. Install breaker arm on pivot pin. Position

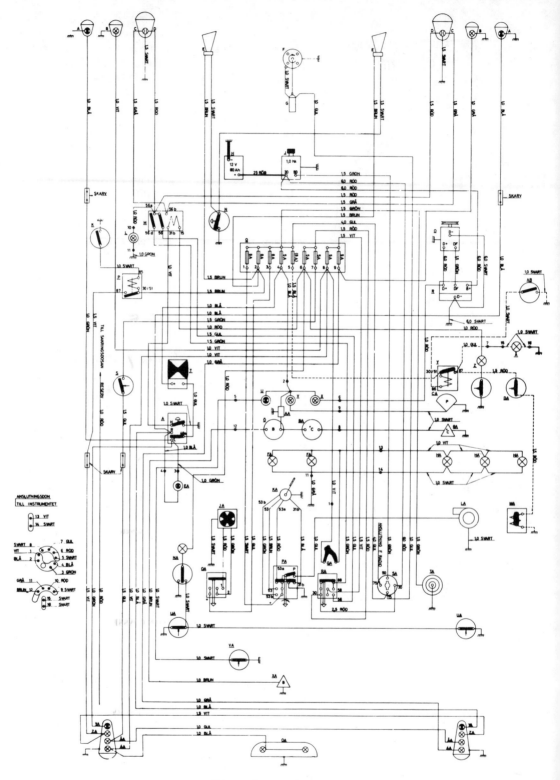

Wiring diagram, Series 144.

A — Direction indicator light 32
    CP
B — Parking light 5 W
C — Dipped light 40 W
D — Fullbeam light 45 W
E — Horn
F — Distributor, firing order
    1-3-4-2
G — Ignition coil
H — Battery 12 V 60 amp/hr
J — Starter motor 1 hp
K — Switch for reversing light
    on gearbox
L — Control lamp for fullbeam
    light 1.2 W
M — Stop relay for fullbeam,
    dipped and headlight
    flasher
N — Horn ring
O — Alternator 12 V 30 A
P — Relay for reversing light
Q — Fuse box
R — Charging control
S — Brake contact
T — Flasher unit
U — Warning light, handbrake,
    1.2 W
V — Warning light, oil pressure,
    1.2 W
X — Warning light, charging,
    1.2 W
Y — Relay for overdrive

Z — Glove compartment light,
    2 W
A — Control lamp for overdrive
    1.2 W
Ä — Switch for light signal and
    direction indicators
Ö — Fuel gauge
AA — Voltage regulator
BA — Temperature gauge
CA — Oil pressure warning unit
DA — Switch for overdrive on
    gearbox
EA — Control lamp flashers
    1.2 W
FA — Instrument lighting 2X3 W
GA — Temperature sending unit
HA — Lighting for heater controls
    3X1.2 W
JA — Heater
KA — Windscreen wipers
LA — Windscreen washer
MA — Solenoid for overdrive
NA — Interior light 10 W
OA — Switch for heater
PA — Switch for windscreen
    wipers and washer
QA — Rheostat for instrument
    lighting
RA — Lighting switch
SA — Ignition switch
TA — Cigarette lighter
UA — Door contact

VA — Switch for handbrake
    control
XA — Fuel gauge tank sender
YA — Flasher light 32 CP
ZA — Reversing light 15 W
AA — Brake light 25 W
ÄA — Rear light 5 W
ÖA — Number plate lighting
    2X5 W
AB — Switch for overdrive

Connections to instruments
13 WHITE   4 BLUE
14 BLACK   3 GREEN
8 BLACK   11 GRAY
1 WHITE   12 BROWN
2 BLUE   10 RED
7 YELLOW   9 BLACK
6 RED   15 BLACK
5 BLACK   16 BLACK

Translation of diagram text
Bla = Blue
Brun = Brown
Gra = Gray
Gul = Yellow
Röd = Red
Svart = Black
Skarv = Junction
Anslutning f. radio = connection
    for radio

spring insulating washer correctly in spring support. Plug-in breaker arm wire. Adjust gap to specifications. Tighten.

Point gap can be set by using a feeler gauge or a dwell meter. Accurate measurements with a feeler gauge require careful, precise usage of the feelers.

A dwell meter should be calibrated first, switched to the four- or six-cylinder position, and connected between distributor primary terminal and ground. Remove distributor cap and rotor. Loosen the breaker set screw approximately ⅛ turn. Observing the dwell meter, reset screw of stationary contact to obtain specific dwell angle. Tighten set screw and recheck dwell. Install rotor and cap, start engine, and make a final dwell angle check.

Ignition Timing

Timing marks are located on the crankshaft pulley and a raised spot is on the timing gear cover. (The B14 and B16 engines have timing marks on the flywheel and a pointer in a window on the right side of the flywheel housing.) Timing is correct when the timing marks are aligned at the moment No. 1 cylinder reaches top dead center.

Basic timing is set by rotating distributor housing counterclockwise slightly until contact points just start to open. Timing marks must line up at this point. Install distributor cap, and connect spark plugs.

Adjust ignition timing after setting point gap. A fast and easy way to adjust timing is with a stroboscope. A second method does not require the strobe light.

Connect strobe light to No. 1 spark plug. Disconnect all vacuum hoses from distributor and plug the hoses. Start engine and reduce idle speed to below 500 rpm. Idle performance must be smooth. Slowing the idle is essential to keep the centrifugal advance in distributor from engaging. Rotate distributor as necessary to align timing marks with strobe pulses.

If strobe light is not available, timing can be adjusted by measuring the advance and retard points with chalk or other marker. Disconnect vacuum hoses from distributor and plug the hoses. Start engine and reduce idle speed to below 500 rpm. When idle performance is smooth, slowly advance the distributor to

point where engine reaches its highest rpm. Mark this point. Next retard the spark by slowly reversing the distributor to the point of lowest rpm. Mark this point. Center the distributor between the two marks and tighten it.

Windshield Wipers

The windshield wipers are driven by an electric motor mounted to the wiper drive linkage under the instrument panel. The motor has two speeds which are selected by a switch on the instrument panel. The windshield washer is operated by a motor driven pump mounted at the bottom of the water container under the hood.

Wiper Assembly Relacement

To replace the wiper assembly, remove wiper arms from shaft. Remove nuts, washers and seals from wiper shafts. Label and remove leads from wiper motor assembly. Remove screw which holds wiper mechanism to the body. This is accessible from the underside of the instrument panel. Install new wiper assembly in reverse order, making sure rubber seals are in good condition. Lubricate nylon bushings on wiper linkage with grease or vaseline. Grease wiper gear housing and lubricate wiper arm shafts with light engine oil.

Horns

Two horns are mounted between the radiator and radiator grille. One horn gives a low note and the other a high note. Depressing the horn ring on the steering wheel closes a relay circuit which provides a ground to complete the horn circuit. If the horn does not operate, check to see that voltage is being supplied to the horn terminal from the fuse block. If the tone of the horn changes, check for loose or otherwise defective mounting.

Lighting

Lights consist of headlamps with high and low beams, flashing directional signals, rear lights, stop lights, back-up lights, parking lights, license plate lights and instrument lights. Switching between high and low beams is by means of a foot switch on the floor which operates a relay mounted on the right side of the engine compartment.

Indicator Lamps

CHARGING INDICATOR

The charging indicator lamp should light when the ignition is turned on and extinguish when the engine is running, indicating that the generator is charging

Light Bulb Specifications

Model	Usage	Wattage or Candle Pr.
122	Headlights	45/40
	Parking	5
	Flashers, Front & Rear	32 CP
	Stop/Tail	32/4 CP
	Backup	15
	License Plate	5
	Interior	10
	Glove Compartment	2
	Instruments	2
	Warning:	
	Turn Signals	2
	Headlight	2
	Charging	2
	Oil Pressure	6
142, 144, 145	Headlights	45/40
	Parking:	
	Front	5
	Rear	4 CP
	Flashers, Front & Rear	32 CP
	Stop	32 CP
	Backup	32 CP
	License Plate	5
	Interior	10
	Glove Compartment	2
	Instruments	3
	Lighting, Heater Controls	1.2
	Warning:	
	Charging	1.2
	Turn Signals	1.2
	Handbrake	1.2
	Headlights	1.2
	Oil Pressure	1.2
	Rear Window Heater	2
164	Headlights	45/40
	Parking	5 (4 CP)
	Flashers, Front & Rear	32 CP
	Rear Lights	5 (4 CP)
	Stop Lights	25 (32 CP)
	Backup	15 (32 CP)
	License Plate	5
	Interior	10
	Glove Compartment	2
	Engine and Luggage Compartments	18
	Instruments	3
	Lighting, Heater Controls	1.2
	Warning:	
	Instrument Panel	1.2
	Overdrive	1.2
	Rear Window Heater	1.2

the battery. If the lamp does not light when the ignition switch is turned on before the engine starts, the lamp and fuse circuit should be checked. If lamp lights while engine is running, the generator charging circuit should be checked.

OIL PRESSURE INDICATOR

The oil pressure indicator lamp is energized through the ignition switch circuit and should light when the ignition switch is turned on to start the engine. The lamp should go out when the engine starts and remain out indicating adequate oil pressure, while it is running. If the lamp should light while the engine is running, stop the engine immediately and check oil pressure.

DIRECTIONAL SIGNAL INDICATORS

Check for defective bulbs if the indicator lamp does not light or flashes abnormally.

HIGH BEAM HEADLIGHT INDICATOR

Indicator for high beam headlights is a blue glow provided by a lamp behind the instrument panel.

HANDBRAKE WARNING LIGHT

Lamp is energized through ignition switch. Automatically lights when brake is applied.

Fuses

Fuses employ melt-type wires and are mounted on a fuse block on the firewall under the hood for the 444, 544 and 122, and on a fuseblock near the heater behind an opening in the protection panel under the dashboard on the 140 and 164 series. If a fuse should blow repeatedly, look for trouble in the electrical circuits and components which it feeds. Do not install a higher current rated fuse.

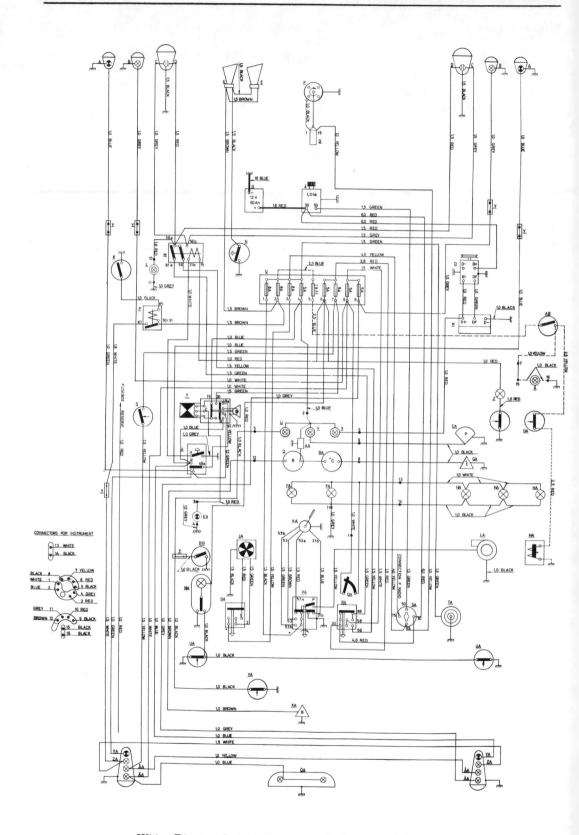

Wiring Diagram, Series 142, 144, standard transmission, 1969–70.

A—Dir. ind. winker 32 CP
B—Parking light 5 W
C—Headlight dipped beam 40 W
D—Headlight main beam 45 W
E—Horn
F—Distributor, firing order
    1-3-4-2
G—Ignition coil
H—Battery 12 V 60 Ah
J—Starter motor 1,0 h.p.
K—Switch for reversing light on
    gearbox
L—Main beam control lamp
    1, 2 W
M—Dipper relay for main and
    dipped beams and
    headlight flasher
N—Horn ring
O—Generator 12 V
P—Relay for reversing light
Q—Fusebox
R—Charging control unit
S—Brake contact

T—Warning flasher
U—Brake control lamp 1, 2 W
V—Oil pressure control lamp
    1, 2 W
X—Charging control lamp 1, 2 W
Y—Junction
Z—Glove compartment
    lighting 2 W
A—Overdrive control lamp 1, 2 W
A—Switch for headlight
    signalling and winkers
O—Fuel gauge
AA—Voltage regulator
BA—Temperature gauge
CA—Oil pressure tell tale
DA—Switch for overdrive on
    gearbox
EA—Winker control lamp 1, 2 W
FA—Instrument lighting 2x3 W
GA—Temperature gauge sensitive
    head
HA—Heater control lighting
    3x1, 2 W

JA—Heater
KA—Windscreen wipers
LA—Windscreen washers
MA—Solenoid for overdrive
NA—Interior lamp 10 W
OA—Switch for heater
PA—Switch for windscreen wipers
    and washer
QA—Instrument lighting rheostat
RA—Light switch
SA—Ignition switch
TA—Cigarette lighter
UA—Door contact
VA—Switch for handbrake control
XA—Fuel gauge tank unit
YA—Winker light 32 CP
ZA—Reversing light 15 W
AA—Brake stoplight 25 W
AA—Tail light 5 W
OA—Number plate lighting 2x5 W
AB—Switch for overdrive
BB—Warning valve

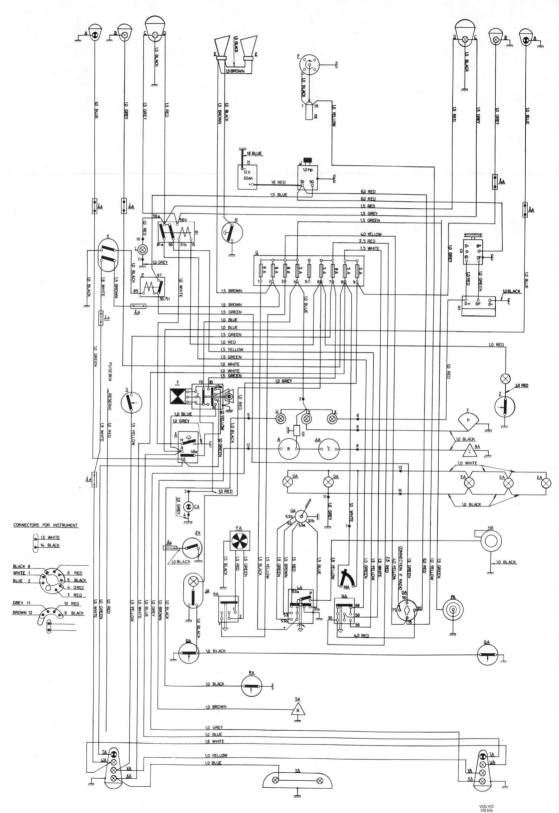

Wiring Diagram, Series 142, 144, automatic transmission, 1969–70.

VOLVO
103 606

A—Dir. ind. winker 32 CP
B—Parking light 5 W
C—Headlight dipped beam 40 W
D—Headlight main beam 45 W
E—Horn
F—Distributor firing order 1-3-4-2
G—Ignition coil
H—Battery 12 V 60 Ah
J—Starter motor 1,0 h.p.
K—Switch unit for starter lockout
    and reversing lights
L—Main beam control lamp
    1, 2 W
M—Dipper relay for main and
    dipped beams and
    headlight flasher
N—Horn ring
O—Generator 12 V
P—Relay for solenoid, on
    starter motor
Q—Fusebox

R—Charging control unit
S—Brake contact
T—Warning flasher
U—Brake control lamp 1, 2 W
V—Oil pressure
    control lamp 1, 2 W
X—Charging control lamp 1, 2 W
Y—Oil pressure tell tale
Z—Glove compartment
    lighting 2 W
A—Switch for headlight
    signalling and winkers
A—Fuel gauge
O—Voltage regulator
AA—Temperature gauge
BA—Temperature gauge
    sensitive head
CA—Winker control lamp 1, 2 W
DA—Instrument lighting 2x3 W
EA—Heater control
    lighting 3x1, 2 W

FA—Heater
GA—Windscreen wipers
HA—Windscreen washers
JA—Interior lamp 10 W
KA—Switch for heater
LA—Switch for windscreen
    wipers and washers
MA—Instrument lighting rheostat
NA—Light switch
OA—Ignition switch
PA—Cigarette lighter
QA—Door contact
RA—Switch for handbrake control
SA—Fuel gauge tank unit
TA—Winker light 32 CP
UA—Reversing light 15 W
VA—Brake stoplight 25 W
XA—Tail light 5 W
YA—Number plate lighting 2x5 W
ZA—Warning valve
AA—Junction

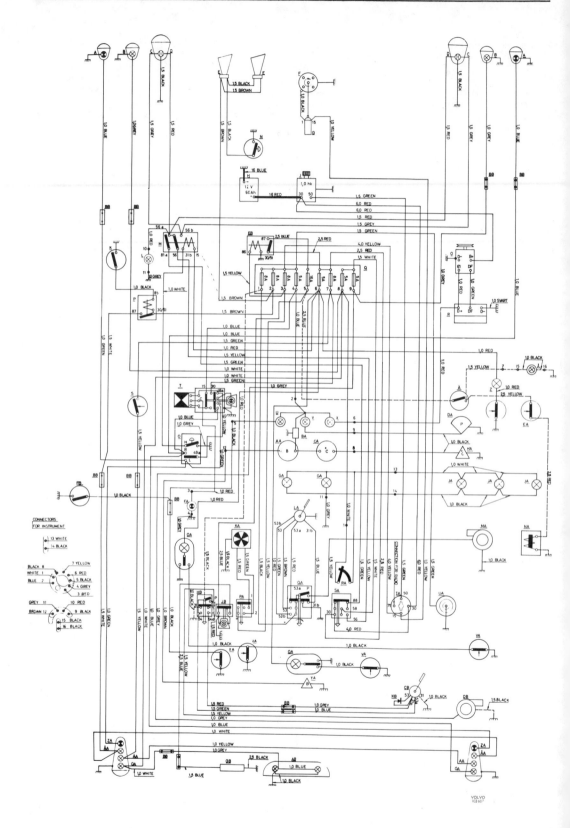

Wiring Diagram, Series 145, standard transmission, 1969–70.

NOTE!
Accessory Parts *—Marked

A Dir. ind. winker 32 CP
B Parking light 5 W
C Headlight dipped beam 40 W
D Headlight main beam 45 W
E Horn
F Distributor firing order 1-3-4-2
G Ignition coil
H Battery 12 V 60 Ah
J Starter motor 1,0 hp
K Switch for reversing light on
   gearbox
L Main beam control lamp
   1, 2 W
M Dipper relay for main and
   dipped beams and headlight
N Horn ring
O Generator 12 V
P Relay for reversing light
Q Fusebox
R Charging control unit
S Brake contact
T Warning flasher
U Handbrake control lamp
   1, 2 W

V Oil pressure control lamp
   1, 2 W
X Charging control lamp 1, 2 W
Y
Z Glove compartment lighting
   2 W
A Control lamp for overdrive
   1, 2 W
A Switch for overdrive
O Switch for headlight
   signalling and winkers
AA Fuel gauge
BA Voltage regulator
CA Temperature gauge
DA Oil pressure tell tale
EA Switch for overdrive on
   gearbox
FA Winker control lamp 1, 2 W
GA Instrument lighting 2x3 W
HA Temperature gauge
   sensitive head
JA Heater control lighting
   3x1, 2 W
KA Heater
LA Windscreen wipers
MA Windscreen washers
NA Solenoid for overdrive

OA Interior lamp 10 W
PA Switch for heater
QA Switch for windscreen
   wipers and washer
RA Instrument lighting rheostat
SA Light switch
TA Ignition switch
UA Cigarette lighter
VA Door contact
XA Switch for handbrake control
YA Fuel gauge tank unit
ZA Winker light 32 CP
AA Reversing light 15 W
AA' Brake stoplight 25 W
OA Tail light 5 W
AB Number plate lighting 2x5 W
BB Skarv
*CB Rear window wiper
*DB Rear window washer
EB Relay for rear window heater
FB Caution contact
GB Heated rear window
*HB Switch for rear window wiper
JB Switch for rear window
   heater with control
   lamp 2 W

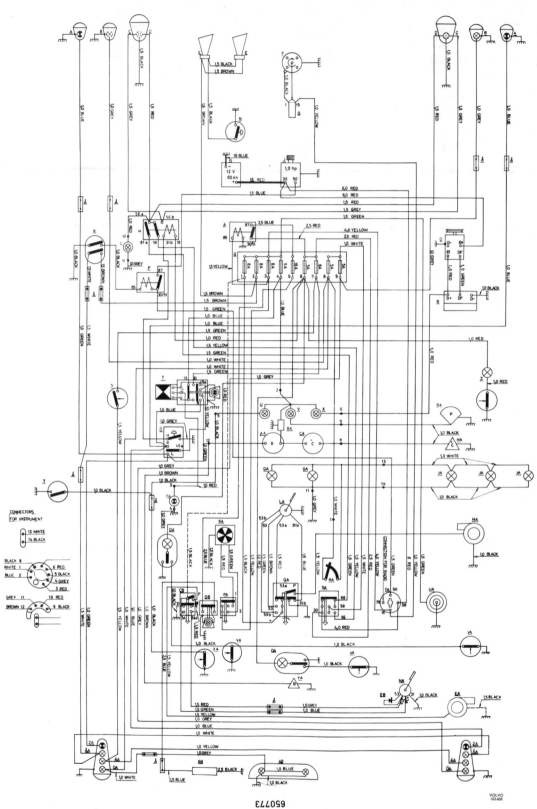

650773

Wiring Diagram, Series 145, automatic transmission, 1969–70.

NOTE!
Accessory Parts *—Marked

A Dir. ind. winker 32 CP
B Parking light 5 W
C Headlight dipped beam 40 W
D Headlight main beam 45 W
E Horn
F Distributor firing order 1-3-4-2
G Ignition coil
H Battery 12 V 60 Ah
J Starter motor 1,0 hp
K Switch unit F starter lockout
   and reversing lights
L Main beam control lamp
   1, 2 W
M Dipper relay for main and
   dipped beams and headlight
N Horn ring
O Generator 12 V
P Relay F solenoid on start
   motor
Q Fusebox
R Charging control unit
S Brake contact

T Warning flasher
U Handbrake control lamp
   1, 2 W
V Oil pressure control lamp
   1, 2 W
X Charging control lamp 1, 2 W
Y Caution contact
Z Glove compartment lighting
   2 W
A Junction
A Relay for rear window heater
O Switch for headlight
   signalling and winkers
AA Fuel gauge
BA Voltage regulator
CA Temperature gauge
DA Oil pressure tell tale
*EA Rear window washer
FA Winker control lamp 1, 2 W
GA Instrument lighting 2x3 W
HA Temperature gauge
   sensitive head
JA Heater control lighting
   3x1, 2 W
KA Heater

LA Windscreen wipers
MA Windscreen washers
*NA Rear window wiper
OA Interior lamp 10 W
PA Switch for heater
QA Switch for windscreen
   wipers and washer
RA Instrument lighting rheostat
SA Light switch
TA Ignition switch
UA Cigarette lighter
VA Door contact
XA Switch for handbrake control
YA Fuel gauge tank unit
ZA Winker light 32 CP
AA Reversing light 15 W
AA Brake stoplight 25 W
OA Tail light 5 W
AB Number plate lighting 2x5 W
BB Heated rear window
*CB Switch for rear window wiper
DB Switch for rear window
   heater with control
   lamp 2 W
*EB Diode

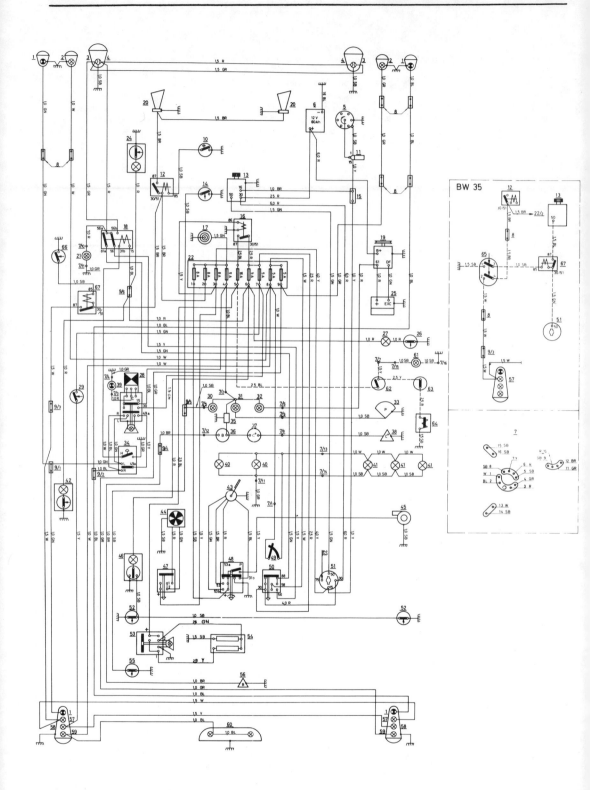

Wiring Diagram, Series 164, 1969–70.

Pos.	Title	Data
1	Dir. ind. flashers	32 cp
2	Parking light	5 W (4 cp)
3	Headlight dipped beam	40 W
4	Headlight main beam	45 W
5	Distributor firing order	1-5-3-6-2-4
6	Battery	12 V 60 Ah
7	Conn. at instrument	
8	Junction	
9	Part of 6-pole conn. unit	
10	Horn ring	
11	Ignition coil	
12	Relay for horn	
13	Starter Motor	1,0 hp.
14	Caution contact	
15	Resistor	
16	Relay for heated rear window	
17	Cigarette lighter	
18	Dipper relay for main and dipped beams and headlight flasher	
19	AC-generator	12 V 35 A
20	Horn	
21	Main beam control lamp	1,2 W
22	Fusebox	
23	Radio connection	
24	Engine comp. lighting	18 W
25	Charging control unit	
26	Switch glove comp. lighting	
27	Glove compartment lighting	2W
28	Warning flashers	
29	Brake contact	
30	Brake control lamp	1,2 W
31	Oil pressure control lamp	1,2 W
32	Charging control lamp	1,2 W
33	Oil pressure tell tale	
34	Switch for headlight-signalling and flashers	
35	Voltage regulator	
36	Fuel gauge	
37	Temperature gauge	
38	Temperature gauge sensitive head	
39	Flashers control lamp	1,2 W
40	Instrument lighting	2x3 W
41	Heater control lighting	3x1,2 W
42	Luggage comp. light	18 W
43	Windscreen wipers	
44	Heater	
45	Windscreen washers	
46	Interior lamp	10 W
47	Switch for heater	
48	Switch for windscreen wipers and washer	
49	Instrument lighting rheostat	
50	Light switch	
51	Ignition switch	
52	Door contact	
53	Switch heat, rear window	
54	Heated rear window	
55	Switch for handbrake control	
56	Fuel gauge tank unit	
57	Reversing light	15 W (32 cp)
58	Brake stoplight	25 W (32 cp)
59	Tail light	.5 W (4 cp)
60	Number plate lighting	2x5 W
61	Overdr. control lamp	1,2 W
62	Switch for overdrive	
63	Switch f. overdr. on gearbox	
64	Solenoid f. overdrive	
65	Switch on gearbox BW 35	
66	Switch for reversing light only for M 400 and M 410	
67	Relay for reversing light on M 400, M 410 and starter relay on BW 35	

Chapter 6
Clutch

Description, Removal and Repair

All Volvo gear shift models use 8″ or 8½″ dry disc type clutches of Borg and Beck manufacture. Clutch control, actuated by the foot pedal, is hydraulic on 122S and 1800S and right-hand drive 164 models and mechanical on 164, 144, PV444, 445, 544 and P210 models. Thrust on the pressure plate is provided by six strong pressure springs on all models except the 164, 145, 144 and 142 which utilize a diaphragm-type spring. Other differences are noted in the specification table.

The clutch for the 142 and 144 Series cars is an 8½″ diaphragm-type spring. This clutch is supplied in two versions, differing mainly in the casing design. The diaphragm spring serves as a clutch lever when disengaging and as the pressure spring when engaging. Clutch action is controlled by a flexible thrust wire instead of a shaft.

Adjusting Clutch Pedal Play
(See Chapter One)

Hydraulic Clutch Control

The 122S, 1800 and right-hand drive 164 have the clutch actuated through the use of an independent hydraulic system for clutch actuation. Pressure on the clutch pedal is transmitted through hydraulic lines from a master cylinder (similar to a brake master cylinder), to a slave cylinder, which operates on the clutch through a thrust rod.

Master Cylinder
To remove the master cylinder, remove

Removing clutch.

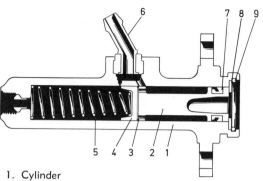

1. Cylinder
2. Piston
3. Washer
4. Piston seal
5. Spring
6. Connection pipe to
    fluid reservoir
7. Piston seal
8. Washer
9. Snap-ring

Hydraulic clutch master cylinder.

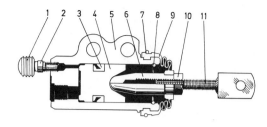

1. Rubber cover
2. Bleeding nipple
3. Piston seal
4. Piston
5. Cylinder
6. Thrust sleeve
7. Snap-ring
8. Stop ring
9. Rubber cover
10. Locknut
11. Thrust rod

Hydraulic clutch slave cylinder.

the hose and drain the fluid reservoir. Disconnect the hydraulic line. Unbolt the cylinder from the pedal and the firewall. To install reverse the procedure, fill the reservoir and bleed the system.

To disassemble the master cylinder, remove the snap-ring and take out the washer, piston, piston seal and return spring. Remove the outer seal from the piston.

Inspect the piston and bore of the cylinder for wear and scoring. Dark marks are caused by the seals and are normal. Small burrs may be removed with emery paper, but if there is major wear, the parts must be replaced.

To assemble the master cylinder, dip the seals and piston in brake fluid and fit the seal to the piston. Insert the spring, piston seal, piston and washer. Insert the snap-ring, and fit the thrust rod and boot. Be sure the vent hole in the boot opens down.

SLAVE CYLINDER

Disconnect the hydraulic line from the cylinder, and the thrust rod from the clutch lever. Unhook the return spring. Remove bolts and lift out. Replace in the reverse procedure. Always bleed the system after the hydraulic line has been replaced.

To disassemble the slave cylinder, remove the rubber cover and thrust rod. Take off the snap-ring and remove the piston.

Inspect the piston and bore of the cylinder for wear and scoring. Dark marks are

caused by the seal and are normal. Small burrs may be removed from the piston with emery paper, but if there is major wear or scoring, the parts must be replaced.

To assemble the slave cylinder, dip the piston and seal in brake fluid and fit the seal on the piston. Insert the piston in the cylinder. Install the snap-ring, thrust rod and boot.

BLEEDING THE SYSTEM

Fill the fluid reservoir with brake fluid. Remove the rubber cap from the bleeder valve on the slave cylinder and attach a hose leading to a jar of brake fluid. Open the valve and depress the clutch pedal. Shut the valve with the pedal depressed and release the pedal. Repeat until the fluid is free of air bubbles. Discard the fluid in the jar and fill the reservoir with fresh fluid.

Clutch Removal

After removing the transmission as described in Chapter Seven, proceed as follows for removal of the clutch assembly. Remove upper bolt from starter motor. Remove the throwout bearing. Disconnect the thrust wire (or linkage) from the housing and release yoke. Remove the flywheel housing. Remove the release yoke by first loosening the ball joint a few turns

1. Facings   3. Spring
2. Hub   4. Disc

Clutch disc.

Test-out disc hub on clutch gear splines for easy slip fit. Do not lubricate.

Check release bearing for wear, binding, or roughness. (NOTE: do not clean disc or release bearing in solvent.) Test pilot-bearing surface on clutch gear spline and check bearing in rear of crankshaft. If necessary, replace bearing.

Clutch Inspection

Cause	Remedy
Clutch Facings Worn Near Rivets	
Improper clutch pedal lash	Replace driven-disc assembly. Adjust clutch pedal lash, ¾"-1"
Pressure Plate Face Badly Scored or Rough	
Improper clutch pedal lash causing pressure plate to contact rivets	Smooth the face with fine emery cloth if possible; otherwise, replace pressure plate and driven disc assemblies.
Heat-Blued Driven-Disc and Pressure Plate Assemblies	
Improper pedal lash	Replace driven disc only. Adjust pedal lash.
Grab and Chatter with Oil Present on Clutch Assembly	
Oil leak	Correct oil leak, clean pressure plate in solvent, replace driven disc and adjust pedal lash.

and holding it while loosening the bolt to which it is attached. The release yoke can then be removed from the rear after turning one-half turn.

Mark the clutch and flywheel by paint or a center punch (if not already marked) so that they can be reassembled in the same relative position. Remove bolts holding clutch to flywheel by alternately loosening opposite bolts a little at a time to prevent warping, while holding clutch so that it does not fall. Remove clutch from bottom.

Clutch Inspection

Inspect clutch parts for wear and damage. Check friction surfaces of flywheel and pressure plate for scoring, ends of release fingers for wear, and clutch facings for wear or oil saturation. Inspect driven disc for distortion (lateral run-out should not exceed .016" at the outer diameter).

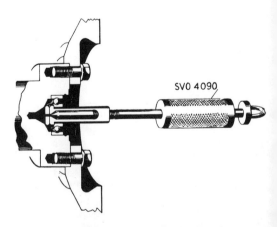

Removing pilot bearing.

Clutch Installation

Before installing, wash flywheel, clutch facings and pressure plate completely free of oil with gasoline and wipe dry with a clean cloth. Observe markings on flywheel and clutch so that they may be aligned properly. Place clutch on flywheel so that longest projection plate hub faces rear. Insert centering mandrel SVO 2484 (SVO 2824 for the 164) so that the guide pin centers the pilot bearing in the flywheel. Install six bolts and tighten opposite bolts a little at a time. Remove mandrel. Install release yoke by placing in flywheel housing back to front and turning one-half turn. Install throwout bearing. Fit and tighten nut for upper starter motor bolt. Install transmission as described in Chapter Seven. Connect pedal linkage. Adjust clutch as described in Chapter One.

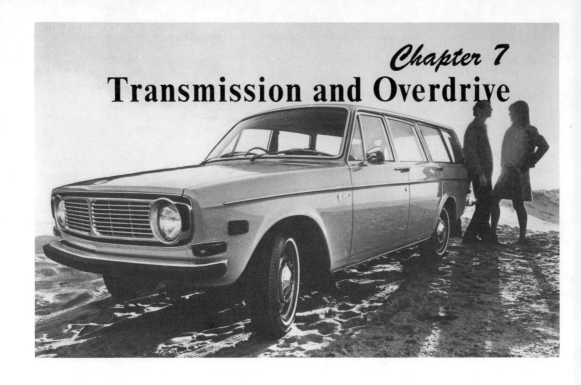

Chapter 7
Transmission and Overdrive

Transmission Specifications

	M4	M30	M40	M400
Gear Ratios				
1st	3.45:1	3.13:1	3.13:1	3.14:1
2nd	2.18:1	1.55:1	1.99:1	1.97:1
3rd	1.31:1	1:1	1.36:1	1.34:1
4th	1:1	–	1:1	1:1
Reverse	3.55:1	3.25:1	3.25:1	3.54:1
Lubricant	SAE 90	SAE 90	SAE 90	
	(Use SAE 80 below 32°F)			
Oil Cap.	1.8 pts.	1.5 pts.	1.5 pts.	1.3 pts
Overdrive	3.5 pts (transmission and			2.95 pts
	overdrive) SAE 20–40			
Reduction Ratio:	.756:1			.797:1

Description, Removal, Disassembly

Transmission

The earliest Volvo transmissions, Types H1 through H6, were three-forward-speed transmissions employing synchronized second and third. The fully synchronized transmissions have type designations M30, M40, and M400. The M30 is a three speed unit and the M40 and M400 are four speed units. The M4 is a synchronized four speed unit with somewhat higher gear ratios in first, second and reverse. The M400 is used only on the 164. Types designated M31, M41 and M410 types are M30 and M40 units equipped with overdrive. All gears, excepting reverse are always in mesh. In neutral, gears on the main shaft rotate freely in bronze bushings. The shifting patterns for the transmissions are identical.

TRANSMISSION REMOVAL

The transmission can be removed from the vehicle after lifting and suspending the engine.

Drain the cooling system and disconnect radiator and heater hoses. Disconnect exhaust pipe at manifold. Disconnect battery cable, oil pressure gauge and throttle controls.

Remove rubber protector and gear shift lever from transmission. Jack up vehicle and place on blocks. Drain oil from transmission. Place jack under transmission to take its weight. Remove supporting member. Disconnect front universal joint (from transmission flange). Disconnect speedometer cable. Disconnect rear engine mounting and bracket for exhaust pipe. Lower the rear end of the engine about ¾" and remove connections for backup lights and overdrive. For B18 engines, remove transmission retaining bolts with a ⅜" socket and swiveling joint (SVO 2427) and pull out the transmission to the rear. For B16 engines, remove these bolts with the help of wrench SVO 2426 and swiveling joint SVO 2427. Then after using SVO 2428 to remove bolts, pull out transmission toward rear.

REPLACING OIL SEAL

The oil seal can be replaced without removal of the transmission after lifting and suspending the engine as described under "Transmission Removal."
With the engine suspended, loosen the transmission flange nut while holding the flange with tool SVO 2409 (M4, M30, M40) or SVO 2837 (M400). Remove the flange or yoke using puller SVO 2261 for flanges

and SVO 2262 for yokes. Remove the old oil seal with puller SVO 4030. Install new seal using sleeve SVO 2413 (M4, M30, M40) or SVO 2412 (M400). Press on flange with SVO 2304 (M4, M30, M40) or SVO 1845 (M400). Install remaining parts.

TRANSMISSION DISASSEMBLY—M4, M30, M40

If the transmission is equipped with overdrive, remove the bolts in rear and overdrive, then proceed with the following.

Mount stand SVO 4109 and jig SVO 2044 in a vise, and place the transmission in this fixture. Remove the transmission cover, springs and interlock balls for the selector rails. Remove cover over selector rails, and remove selector fork bolts. For the M30, slide the selector fork backwards and to the reverse position and drive out the pin. For the M40, slide the fork backward to the reverse position. Drive out the pin slightly (do not foul 1st gear wheel). Then move selector fork forward sufficiently to allow the pin to pass in front of the

Removing drive flange.

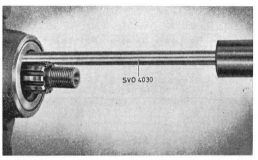

Removing oil seal.

Removing reverse gear.

gear wheel. Drive out the pin. Slide out the selector rails, guiding the selector forks so they do not jam on the rails. Remove the selector forks.

Remove the bolts holding the rear cover, and turn the cover so that it does not lock the shaft for the idler and reverse gears (early production only). Drive out the shaft for the idler gear. (NOTE: the shaft must not be driven out backwards). Let the idler gear fall into the bottom of the transmission.

Pull out the mainshaft. Remove bolts and cover over input shaft. Pry oil seal from cover. Drive out input shaft. If necessary, remove lock ring and press ball bearing off the shaft. Remove idler gear. Pull out shaft for the reverse gear with puller SVO2301. Remove reverse gear and other parts.

MAINSHAFT DISASSEMBLY

For M31 and M41 transmissions, remove the lock ring and press off the rotor for the overdrive oil pump. Remove lock ring for the mainshaft rear bearing and slide forward the engaging sleeve for first and second speeds (first and reverse for M31). Place the shaft in a press out shaft.

For M30 and M40 transmissions, remove flange (or yoke), using puller SVO 2261 for flange and SVO 2262 for yoke. Slide forward the engaging sleeves for first and second speeds (first and reverse for M30). Place shaft in a press and press out the shaft with a drift. Remove thrust washer, sleeves, springs and snap springs from shaft. Remove lock ring on front end of shaft. Pull off synchronizing hub and third speed gear wheel (second speed gear wheel on M30) with a puller. Remove the thrust washer. Remove the lock ring, thrust washer, second speed gear wheel (first speed gear wheel for M30), synchronizing cone and spring. Remove oil seals

from rear cover and speedometer gear. If necessary, remove lock ring and press out ball bearing. Assemble mainshaft in reverse order from above.

TRANSMISSION ASSEMBLY

Install reverse gear, making sure that the groove in the reverse shaft (early production) is turned correctly. The reverse shaft for late production models is installed so that it projects .3″ outside the transmission housing.

Place mandrel SVO 2303 in the idler gear. Insert spacing washers and needles (24 in each bearing), using grease to hold the needles and washers in position. Hold the washer to the housing with grease and guide them into position with centering plugs SVO 2302. Lay idler gear in the bottom of the housing.

Press the bearing onto the input shaft using drift SVO 2412. Select a lock ring of proper thickness and install it. Install 14 roller bearings using grease to hold rollers in place. Press input shaft into position. Press oil seal into cover with drift SVO 2010. Install cover using O-rings for bolts (late production). Place mainshaft in housing, turning rear cover so that countershaft can be installed.

Turn transmission upside down to install countershaft from rear. Hold against SVO 2303 with the hand, being careful that the thrust washers do not loosen and

SVO 2412

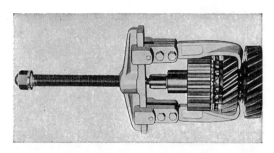

Removing front synchronizer.   Installing ball bearing on input shaft.

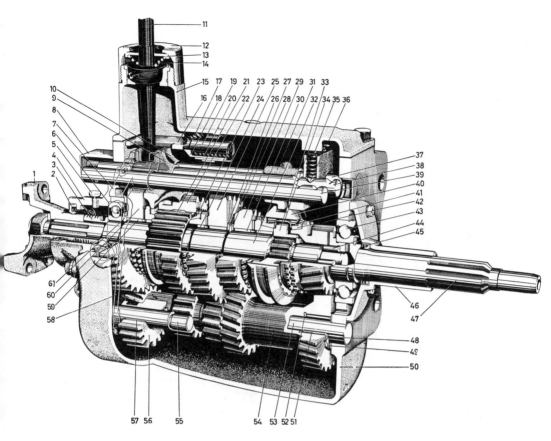

1. Flange
2. Oil seal
3. Speedometer worm gear
4. Rear cover
5. Breather nipple
6. Ball bearing
7. Striker (cutaway view)
8. End casing
9. Selector fork, 1st and 2nd gears
10. Striker
11. Gear lever
12. Cover
13. Washer
14. Spring
15. Cover
16. Sliding plate
17. Spring
18. Sleeve (reverse catch)
19. Sleeve
20. Spring
21. Engaging spring

22. Engaging sleeve and gear wheel for reverse
23. Synchronizing cone
24. Bushing
25. Gear wheel for 2nd gear
26. Thrust washer
27. Lock ring
28. Thrust washer
29. Gear wheel for 3rd gear
30. Bushing
31. Selection fork, 3rd and 4th gears
32. Mainshaft
33. Synchronizing hub
34. Engaging spring
35. Spring
36. Interlock ball
37. Selection rail for 3rd and 4th gears
38. Selection rail for 1st and 2nd gears
39. Selector rail for reverse

40. Engaging sleeve
41. Snap ring
42. Synchronizing cone
43. Ball bearing
44. Roller bearing
45. Oil seal
46. Front cover
47. Input shaft
48. Spacing washer
49. Thrust washer
50. Housing
51. Needle bearing
52. Spacing washer
53. Countershaft
54. Idle gear
55. Reverse shaft
56. Reverse gear
57. Bushing
58. Striker lever (cutaway view)
59. Bushing
60. Gear wheel for 1st gear
61. Thrust washer

M40 transmission.

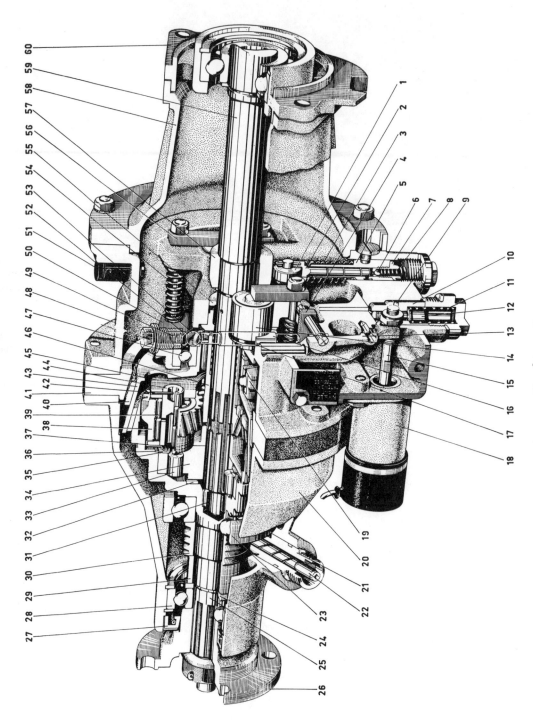

Overdrive unit.

fall. Next turn the rear cover so that it locks the reverse shaft and install the cover bolts. For overdrive types, make sure that the cam for the overdrive oil pump is turned upwards. Install the overdrive. Use new lock washers for the intermediate flange.

Install selector rails and forks. Move selector fork to rear position and install new pin. Install cover over selector rails. (NOTE: if the end caps at front of housing have been removed, they should be installed as before, with center and cap projecting about 5/32" outside the housing.) Place interlock balls and springs in position. Install cover. Check that all gears engage and disengage freely. Install transmission in reverse order to removal. Fill with transmission lubricant.

Transmission Disassembly—M400

Remove the overdrive unit if so equipped. Mount the transmission in stand and jig SVO 2520 and SVO 2825 or equivalent. Remove the cover, springs and interlock balls for the selector rails. Remove the flange using wrench SVO 2837 and puller SVO 2261. Remove the release bearing. Remove the cover for the input shaft and the clutch

housing. Turn the gearbox upside down and pull out the front bearing for the intermediate shaft with tool SVO 2826. Remove the rear cover and pull out the rear bearing of the intermediate shaft with tool SVO 2827.

Turn the gearbox upright, but be careful that the teeth of the intermediate shaft are not damaged as it drops to the bottom of the gearbox. Unscrew the bolts for the selector forks. Push the selector rails backward and drive out the tensioning pin in the flange of the selector rails and the selector rails. Hold the forks while removing the rails so they do not jam as the rails are removed and then remove the forks.

Remove the speedometer gear. Pull out the rear bearing of the mainshaft with tool SVO 2828. For the M410, remove the bolt in the puller and replace it with SVO 2832 and pull out the bearing.

Pull out the input shaft and remove the synchronizing ring. Remove the thrust washer from the mainshaft rear end. Fit lifting tool SVO 2829 or a rope or sling on the mainshaft. Push the engaging sleeve for 1st and 2nd gear rearward and lift out the mainshaft. Pull out the reverse shaft with puller SVO 2830. Remove the oil seals.

1. Roller	21. Bushing	41. Brake drum
2. Pump lunger	22. Speedometer gear, small	42. Locking pin
3. Spring	23. Ball bearing	43. Clutch disc
4. Lever	24. Thrust washer	44. Shaft
5. Pump cylinder	25. Output shaft	45. Planet gear carrier
6. Ball	26. Coupling flange	46. Sunwheel
7. Valve seating	27. Sealing ring	47. Ball bearing
8. Spring	28. Ball bearing	48. Housing, front part
9. O ring	29. Spacing sleeve	49. Plug over control valve
10. Valve seating, relief valve	30. Speedometer gear, large	50. Pressure plate
11. Spring	31. Needle bearing	51. Breather nipple
12. Valve plunger	32. Thrust washer	52. Tappet (cutaway)
13. Lever	33. Freewheel rollers	53. Ball (cutaway)
14. Piston	34. Freewheel hub	54. Spring
15. Armature for solenoid	35. Oil deflector plate	55. Bushing
16. Valve rod (cutaway view)	36. Lock ring	56. Pressure plate
17. Plunger seal	37. Oil catcher	57. Cam
18. Solenoid	38. Planet gear	58. Extension piece
19. Thrust bearing retainer	39. Needle bearing	59. Input shaft (mainshaft)
20. Housing, rear part	40. Clutch facing	60. Rear cover, gearbox

Mainshaft Disassembly

Remove the 1st speed gear, needle bearing and synchronizer cone. Remove the engaging sleeves and flanges for the synchronizers. Remove the snap-rings from the synchronizer hub. With tool SVO 2853 or equivalent, press off the 2nd speed gear and the 1st and 2nd speed synchronizer hub. Turn the shaft over and press off the 3rd speed gear and the 3rd and 4th speed synchronizer hub. Assemble the mainshaft in the reverse order of the above procedure.

Transmission Assembly

Insert front and rear oil seals into the front and rear covers. Press the ball bearing onto the input shaft with tool SVO 2851 and SVO 2852 or equivalent. Fit a snap-ring into the groove. Place the lever for the reverse shaft onto the bearing pin. Fit the reverse gear and shaft. The reverse shaft should be flush within 0.08 in. (0.2 mm.) of the rear of the housing.

Place the intermediate shaft in the bottom of the gearbox housing. Fit the mainshaft in the housing and install a thrust washer. Press the ball bearing onto the mainshaft using press SVO 2831 or equivalent.

Fit the needle bearing in the input shaft. Install the loose synchronizer cone in the 3rd and 4th speed synchronizer hub. Align the flanges in the grooves. Push the input shaft into the housing and onto the pin of the mainshaft.

Turn the gearbox upside down and insert the intermediate shaft bearing with tool SVO 2831 or equivalent. Fit the clutch housing with a new gasket. Turn the gearbox right side up and install the selector forks, flanges and rails. Make sure the flange for the reverse gear fits correctly in the gear lever. Fit the bolts and new tensioning pins.

With the rear end of the gearbox facing up, push the intermediate shaft forward so the front bearing lies against the clutch housing. Fit shims under the intermediate shaft bearing to give a clearance of from 0.002 in. (0.05 mm.) below to even with the rear of the case. Fit the speedometer gear and rear cover with new gasket. Clearance between the intermediate shaft and the rear cover is 0.008 to 0.010 in. (0.2 to 0.25 mm.). Press on the flange with tool SVO 1845, and install the washer and nut to 80 to 110 ft. lbs. (11 to 14 kgm.) of torque. Place the interlocking balls and springs in position. Replace the gearbox and front cover with new gaskets.

Overdrive

Overdrive for the M31 and M40 transmissions is of the planetary gear type and is mounted on the rear end of the transmission. In driving forward, power from the transmission mainshaft is transmitted through the freewheel rollers to the overdrive output shaft. When reversing or using the engine as a brake, power is transmitted through the clutch disc which is held by spring pressure against the tapered portion of the output shaft. In overdrive, the clutch disc is pressed against the brake drum, in which position the sun wheel is locked. When driving, the planet gears rotate around the sun wheel. As a result, the output shaft rotates at higher speed than the mainshaft.

Overdrive is actuated by a switch under the steering wheel or on the instrument panel. This switch energizes a solenoid on the overdrive unit via a switch on the transmission, which is cut in when the 4th speed is engaged. The solenoid has two windings, a heavy control winding and a lower current, "hold" winding. The control winding causes the solenoid to open a valve, whereupon the control winding is cut off and the valve is held open by the hold winding. The valve controls the flow of oil pressure from a cam-operated pump to hydraulic cylinders which operate the overdrive clutch disc.

Overdrive Removal

Remove transmission as described previously. Drain oil from overdrive and disconnect cable to solenoid. Remove bolts which hold overdrive to intermediate flange and remove overdrive unit. Replace unit in reverse order and fill with lubricant. Since specialized testing equipment and tools are required for servicing the overdrive unit, it is best to have a qualified Volvo service department do any repair work necessary.

Chapter 8

Drive Shaft and Rear Axle

Drive Shaft

The drive shaft for the Volvo PV444 up to chassis number 2505 is in one piece. Starting with chassis number 2506 on the PV 444, and for the PV 445, 544, P 210, 144 and 164, the drive shaft is made in two pieces and has three Hardy-Spicer universal joints equipped with needle bearings.

DRIVE SHAFT REMOVAL

The front and rear sections of the drive shaft can be removed in one piece by disconnecting the universal joints at the transmission and at the rear axle, and then pulling the two sections out backwards at the same time. However, to remove either the rear or front section, or both, the following procedure is used.

Disconnect front universal joint of rear section of drive shaft by removing the four bolts in the flange behind the support bearing. Be careful not to drop end of shaft, for it can be damaged easily. Disconnect rear universal joint at pinion driving flange in the same manner, and remove rear section of drive shaft.

After the rear section has been removed, punch mating marks on flange and shaft and disconnect the front universal of the front section by removing the bolts from the flange of the transmission shaft. The drive shaft with universal joint and bearing housing can then be removed by pulling out backwards.

DRIVE SHAFT DISASSEMBLY

If front and rear sections of shaft are assembled, bend back tabs of lock washer and remove nut for support bearing. Remove rear section of shaft. Pull off the support bearing.

UNIVERSAL JOINT DISASSEMBLY

Remove lock rings which hold needle bearings in the yokes. Tighten shaft in vise being careful not to deform it. With a hammer and thick steel punch, drive the spider as far as it will go in the opposite direction. The needle bearing will then come about half way out. Then drive the spider as far as it will go in the other direction. Drive out one of the needle bearings with a thinner punch. Remove the spider and then drive out the other needle bearing.

Inspect the shaft. It must be straight, or it can cause vibration. An indicator gauge should be used for checking while the

117

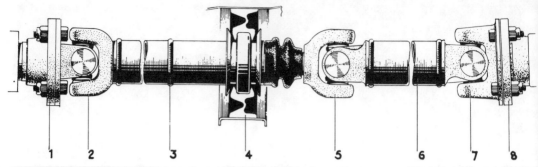

1. Transmission flange
2. Front universal
3. Front section of drive shaft

4. Support bearing
5. Intermediate universal

6. Rear section of drive shaft
7. Rear universal
8. Rear axle flange

Drive shaft components.

1. Driving flange
2. Bearing housing
3. Splash guard
4. Center punch
5. Bolt

Marking drive shaft and flange.

Removing needle bearings.

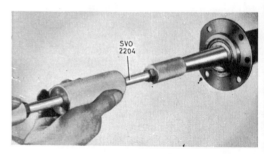

Removing rear axle.

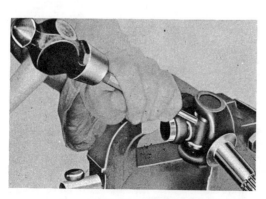

Removing spider.

Removing rear axle oil seal.

shaft is rotated. If it is out by more than .010″ the shaft must be replaced. No attempt should be made to straighten a bent shaft.

Examine support bearing by pressing races toward each other with the hand and turning them in opposite directions. If the bearing binds or does not run easily, replace it. Check needle bearings and spiders for wear or damage.

DRIVE SHAFT ASSEMBLY

Check that needle bearings are half-filled with grease. Insert spider in flange yoke, pushing the spider over in one direction far enough so that needle bearing can be installed onto trunnion. Then with a drift, press in needle bearing so that lock ring can be inserted. Install other needle bearings and spiders in the same way. Install drive shaft on vehicle in reverse order to removal.

Rear Axle

Hypoid gears are employed in PV 544, P 1800, P 120, 144S, 164 and in PV 444, starting with Chassis 8378. The principle of rear axle suspension is utilized. Each axle is supported at its outer end by a tapered bearing. Differential bearing lateral adjustment is made by inserting or removing shims between the housing and the differential side bearings. Axle end play is determined by shims between the brake backing plate and the end of the axle housing.

Rear axle shafts, bearings, oil seals and the pinion oil seal at the front of the housing can be replaced without removing the axle and rear housings from the vehicle.

AXLE, OIL SEAL AND WHEEL BEARING REPLACEMENT

Remove wheel and pull off wheel hub. Avoid getting oil or grease on brake linings. Place a wooden block under the brake pedal and disconnect brake line from backing plate.

Pull axle, using puller SVO 2204. Remove oil seal with puller SVO 4078. Drive in new oil seal, making sure it is correctly positioned.

Press off bearing, using SVO 1806 under the bearing. Install new bearing with SVO 1805 and pack with grease. Remove any oil or grease from the brake

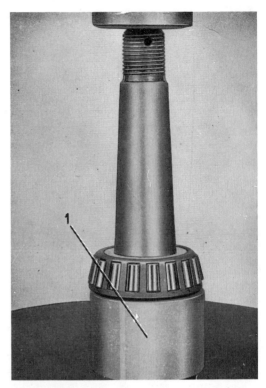

Removing rear axle bearing. 1 = Tool SVO 1806.

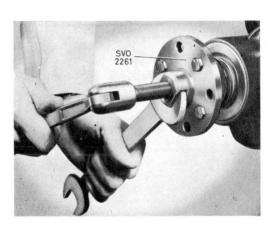

Removing pinion flange.

backing plate. Install axle and brake backing plate with a new felt washer. Replace draw key if it has been removed, and install hub and wheel. Bleed brake lines and adjust brakes. Check oil level in rear, and add oil if necessary.

PINION OIL SEAL REPLACEMENT

Disconnect rear section of drive shaft from pinion flange. Remove flange nut using SVO 2409 as a counterhold. Pull flange with SVO 2261. Remove old oil seal with SVO 4030 and install new oil seal with new paper gasket using tool SVO 2403. Press on flange with SVO 1845 and install washer and nut. Tighten to a torque of 200-220 lb.-ft. Reconnect drive shaft.

Axle and Rear Housing Removal

Place blocks in front of the front wheels. Drain rear. Loosen rear wheel nuts. Place special rear axle fixture SVO 2714 on a heavy-duty jack and lift under rear hous-ing. Place supports under body slightly forward of rear wheels. Remove rear flange on rear. Disconnect brake line from master cylinder (place wooden block under brake pedal). Disconnect hand-brake cables and brackets on brake backing plate. Loosen track bar, upper shock absorber bolts and shock absorber straps from axle. Loosen nuts for support arms. Lower the rear axle and remove springs. Loosen bolts for torque rods and remove rear axle. Clean rear axle externally and allow oil to drain off.

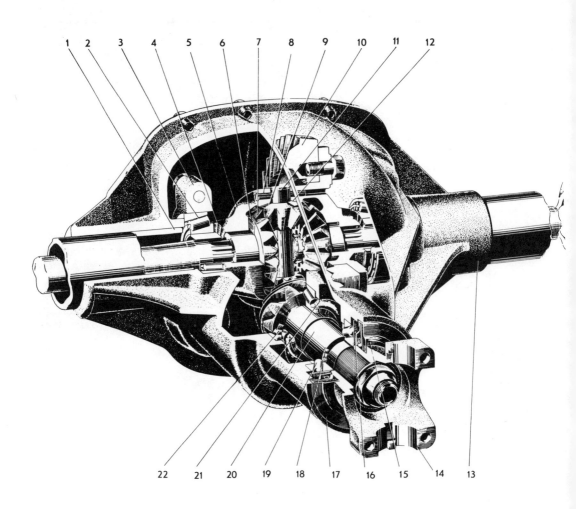

1. Tubular shaft	9. Differential pinion	16. Oil slinger
2. Differential shaft	10. Ring gear	17. Pinion oil seal
3. Bearing cap	11. Shaft	18. Shims
4. Shims	12. Thrust washer	19. Front pinion bearing
5. Differential carrier	13. Axle housing	20. Pinion
6. Thrust washer	14. Pinion flange	21. Rear pinion bearing
7. Differential gear	15. Dust cover plate	22. Shims
8. Lock pin		

Rear axle and differential (144).

Wheels, Suspension, Steering
Chapter 9

Description, Removal and Repair

The front end of the Volvo employs independent front wheel suspension with coil springs. Support is provided by upper and lower control arms pivoted on a front axle member bolted to the frame or body. The upper and lower arms support the shock absorber, and the lower arm and front axle members support the coil spring. The steering knuckle is carried in king pins between the arms. Stabilizer bars are attached to the lower control arm and frame. Coil springs are used also in the rear.

Front Wheel Suspension

Front Wheel Alignment

(See Chapter Two—"Front End Troubleshooting")

Wheel Bearing Replacement

(Tools for PV 444, 445, 544, and P210 are shown in parenthesis). Loosen wheel nuts slightly before jacking, then jack up front end and place blocks under the lower control arms. Remove wheel. For 164 and 144 models, remove brake caliper by disconnecting brake lines and removing mounting bolts. Remove grease cap, cotter pin and wheel nut. Pull hub with SVO 2726 (SVO 1791, 1446). Pull inner bearing from wheel axle with SVO 2722 (SVO 1794, 4016) if the bearing remains in place. Remove inner bearing race with drift SVO 2724 (SVO 1799, 4003) and outer clearing race with drift SVO 2725 (SVO 1800, 4002) together with handle SVO 1801. Clean hub, grease cap, brake disc and drum.

Press in new bearings with drift SVO 2723 (SVO 1798, 4001) for the inner race and SVO 2724 (SVO 1797, 4000) for the outer race together with handle SVO 1801. Pack bearings full of grease, applying grease to outer sides of bearings and on outer races pressed into hub. Fill recess in hub with grease all around up to the smallest diameter of the outer race on the outer bearing. Insert inner bearing into position in hub and press in seal with SVO 2723 (SVO 1798, 4001) and handle SVO 1801. Place hub on axle. Install outer bearing, washer and wheel nut.

Adjust wheel bearings by first tighten-

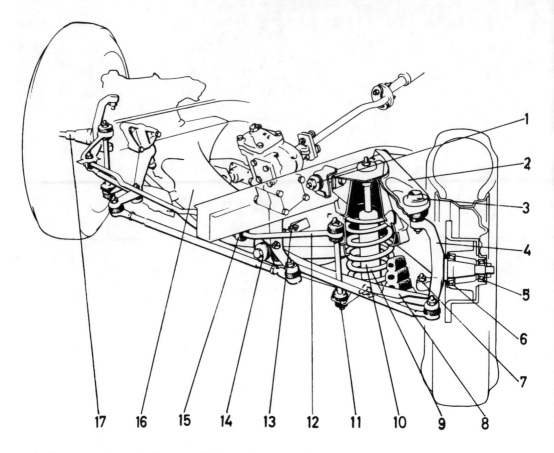

1. Upper control arm bushing	7. Lower control arm ball joint	12. Stabilizer
2. Upper control arm	8. Lower control arm	13. Stop screw max. wheel lock
3. Upper control arm ball joint	9. Coil spring	14. Lower control arm bushing
4. Steering knuckle	10. Shock absorber	15. Frame attachment for stabilizer
5. Outer wheel bearing	11. Stabilizer attachment	16. Front axle member
6. Inner wheel bearing		17. Front wheel axle

Front suspension, 144.

ing wheel nut to a torque of 50 lbs. ft. Then loosen nut one-third turn and install cotter pin. Check that wheel rotates easily without play. Half fill the grease cap and install. Install brake caliper and connect brake lines. Install wheel and tighten wheel nuts.

KING PIN REPLACEMENT

Loosen wheel nuts slightly, and then jack up front end and place blocks under the lower control arms. Remove wheel and wheel hub as described previously under "Wheel Bearing Replacement," removing inner bearing race if necessary. Remove four bolts that hold brake backing plate in place and splash guard to

steering knuckle. Lift off brake backing plate and tie up to avoid straining brake line.

Remove cotter pin and nut from steering arm ball joint. Place SVO 2294 on the ball joint, making sure the thread of the ball joint enters the countersink in the tool. Turn tensioning screw until ball joint releases. Loosen nut and unscrew upper control arm bolt. Remove clamping bolt and eccentric bushing. Disconnect shock absorber at bottom. Lift off steering knuckle support. Screw out lower bushing.

Drive out king pin stop key, and remove sealing washer with a pointed punch. Drive king pin downwards and

1. Steering knuckle support
2. Upper control arm
3. Steering gear housing
4. Stabilizer

5. Pitman arm
6. Front axle member
7. Steering rod and tie rod
8. Lower control arm

9. Coil spring
10. Shock absorber
11. Steering knuckle
12. Steering arm

Front suspension, 544.

Removing inner wheel bearing.

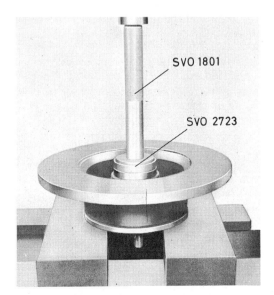

Installing inner wheel bearing seal.

out with SVO 2224. Remove grease fittings and drive out king pin bushings with SVO 1442.

Press in new bushings with SVO 1442. Make sure lubricating holes line up with grease fitting holes, and that the short lubricating groove faces the sealing washer. Ream bushings with SVO 1171. Install grease fittings. Coat bushings with chassis grease.

Position the axle steering knuckle, thrust bearing and adjusting shims, and place the centering mandrel SVO 4005 in the upper bushing. Change shims until the takeup corresponds to a friction torque of 4.34–56.4 lb. in. when turning the axle. This would be a reading of 0.66–9.46 lbs. on a spring scale attached to the cotter pin hole in the axle and pulled at right angles to the axle. Drive in king pin, making sure of correct position. Insert stop key. Check to see that steering knuckle turns easily. Install sealing washers with convex side out, then knock them flat with a hammer and drift pin.

Install steering knuckle support with bushings, guard plate and bolts. Connect steering rod to steering arm. Turn ball joint so that cotter pin hole lines longitudinally with rod. Tighten castle nut to a torque of 23-27 lb. ft. Install brake backing plate and splash plate on steering knuckle. Install hub and wheel, reversing previous steps for removal. Adjust wheel bearings and check front wheel alignment.

<h3 style="text-align:center">UPPER ARM, BALL JOINT REPLACEMENT (164, 144)</h3>

Jack up front end of vehicle and remove wheel. Loosen nut for upper control arm ball joint. With a hammer, tap the axle around the ball joint pin until it is loosened from the axle. Remove nut completely and suspend upper end of axle to avoid

straining brake lines. Loosen control arm nuts one-half turn, lift arm slightly and press out ball joint with SVO 2699 and sleeve SVO 2701.

Before installing new ball joint, see that rubber cover is filled with grease. Bend the pin end over the slot, and be sure that the grease forces its way out. Press ball joint into control arm with SVO 2699, sleeve SVO 2701 and drift 2704, making sure that slot in ball joint lines up longitudinally with shaft of control arm either externally or internally, for the pin has maximum movement in the direction of this line. Should the ball joint be incorrectly positioned, turn the tool half a turn and then press the ball joint into the right position. Turn down the control arm and tighten the nuts on the control arm shaft. Tighten ball joint against axle. If the pin rotates, hold it with a C-clamp. Install front wheel.

<h3 style="text-align:center">LOWER ARM, BALL JOINT REPLACEMENT (164, 144)</h3>

Jack up front end of vehicle and remove wheel. Disconnect steering rod from steering arm with SVO 2294, and disconnect brake lines from stabilizer bolt. Slightly loosen nuts on upper and lower ball joints. With a hammer, tap ball joints loose from axle. Raise lower control arm with a jack. Remove nuts. Remove steering knuckle with hub and front wheel brake unit, and place the assembly on an elevated support near enough to avoid

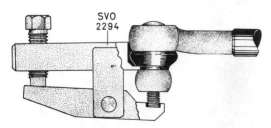
Removing steering rod ball joint.

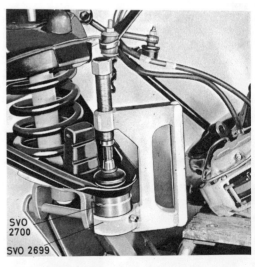
Removing ball joint, upper control arm.

strain on brake lines. Using tools SVO 2699 and SVO 2700, press ball joint out of lower arm. Before installing new joint, check to see that rubber cover is filled with grease by breaking the pin to the side, forcing the grease out. Fill with grease if necessary. Press new ball joint into position in control arm. Install steering knuckle and tighten upper and lower ball joints. Install steering rod, connect brake lines to stabilizer bolt and install front wheel.

Front Spring and Shock Absorber Replacement (164, 144)

Jack front end of vehicle and place on blocks. Remove shock absorber by removing upper nut, washer and rubber bushing. Remove two screws at bottom on underside of lower control arm and take out shock absorber.

Disconnect steering rod from steering arm and loosen clamp for brake lines. Remove stabilizer attachment. Place a jack under the lower control arm. Loosen nuts on ball joints, and tap with hammer until ball joints loosen from wheel axle. Remove nuts. Remove steering knuckle with front wheel brake. Lower jack and remove spring. Install new spring in reverse order of above.

Front Spring Replacement (PV 444, 544)

Jack front end of vehicle and place on blocks. Disconnect stabilizer. Place jack under lower control arm, and loosen four nuts on front axle support member bracket. Lower jack slowly and remove spring. Install new spring in reverse order of above, making sure that new ring is in correct position, with the straight end resting in the recess in the lower spring attachment. Check front wheel alignment and if necessary readjust (See Chapter Two).

Rear Suspension

Rear Spring and Shock Absorber Replacement

Chock front wheels, jack rear of vehicle and place on blocks. Remove rear wheel. Jack up rear axle so that spring is slightly compressed. Loosen upper and lower spring attachments. Remove upper attachment for shock absorber. (Remove lower

attachment also if removing shock absorber). Lower jack carefully and remove spring. Install new rear spring, taking previous steps in reverse order.

Steering Gear Assembly

The steering column of the 140 series has a break-away flange between the upper and lower steering column sections, which shears in the event of a frontal impact on the car. The 164 steering column has a break-away flange at the steering box which shears in the case of a frontal impact, and a sleeve in the column which collapses to absorb impact on the steering column.

Power Steering (164)

The optional 164 ZF power steering unit consists of a steering box, a pump, and a fluid reservoir. The power steering lowers the steering effort and reduces the number of turns of the steering wheel to 3.7 turns lock to lock.

Check the fluid level in the reservoir every 6000 miles. If it is lower than ¼ in. above the level mark, fill with automatic transmission oil, type A. Total capacity of the system is 2.5 pints (1.2 liters).

Since specialized testing equipment and tools are required for servicing the power steering unit, it is best to have a qualified Volvo service department do any repair work necessary.

Volvos employ several different types of steering systems which may be classified as either "cam or lever" or "cam and roller." The 144 employs the cam and roller type, while early production PV 444 and 445 employ the cam and lever types. Depending upon vehicle and steering gear model, the turning circle is about 33 feet. Ball joints not provided with grease fittings are plastic lined and require no lubrication.

Steering Wheel Replacement

Remove horn fuse. Remove screw from the top of the direction indicator switch housing and lift off the housing. Remove screw from top of steering wheel housing, lift up horn ring and remove. Remove steering wheel nut. Make sure direction indicator switch is in the neutral position, and with puller SVO 2711 (164, 140), SVO 2368 (PV 444/445), or SVO 2325 (PV 544, P 210) and the wheels pointed forward, remove steering wheel. When installing new

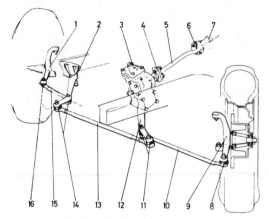

1. Steering knuckle
2. Relay arm
3. Steering gear housing
4. Lower steering column flange
5. Lower steering column section
6. Upper steering column flange
7. Upper steering column section
8. Ball joint
9. Steering knuckle
10. Steering rod
11. Ball joint
12. Pitman arm
13. Tie rod
14. Ball joint
15. Steering rod
16. Ball joint

Steering gear, 144.

steering wheel, tighten to torque of 23–35 ft. lbs. Replace horn fuse.

STEERING ROD AND TIE ROD RECONDITIONING

Bent or otherwise damaged steering rods and tie rods must be replaced, not straightened. Ball joints cannot be disassembled or adjusted, so they must also be replaced when worn or damaged. Steering rod ball joints are made with the rod, so the complete rod and ball joint assembly must be replaced. If the steering rod is to be removed, first remove the ball joint on the pitman arm and idler arm using the procedure described under "King Pin Replacement." Tie rod ball joints can be replaced individually and the same procedure can be used.

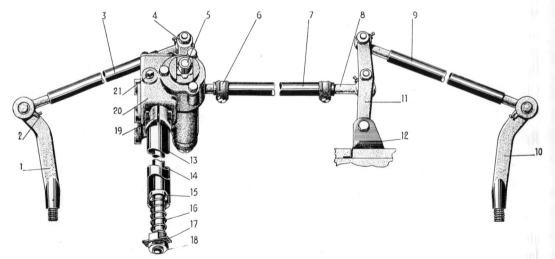

1. Left steering arm	8. Ball joint	15. Ball bearing
2. Grease nipple	9. Right steering rod	16. Spring
3. Left steering rod	10. Right steering arm	17. Locking washer
4. Pitman arm	11. Idler arm	18. Nut
5. Adjusting screw	12. Bracket for idler arm	19. Clamp for housing
6. Clamp	13. Steering column housing	20. Steering gear housing
7. Tie rod	14. Steering column	21. Grease plug

Steering gear, PV444, 445, 544, P210.

Chapter 10

Brakes

Description, Removal and Repair

Model P1800, 1800S and 122S have front wheel disc brakes and drum brakes at the rear, while the 144 and 142 have disc brakes on all four wheels. The PV 544 model employs drum brakes on all four wheels.

Disc Brakes

The disc type system consists of a brake disc which rotates with the wheel and a caliper having a hydraulic cylinder and piston on each side of the disc. The caliper presses friction pads against the disc to stop the car.

BRAKE PAD INSPECTION

Disc brake friction pads can be checked for wear using a gauge that measures the distance from the inside of one friction pad backing plate to the other when the brake is engaged. Brake pads should be replaced if worn down to a thickness of ¹⁄₁₆″.

BRAKE PAD REPLACEMENT

Jack up wheel and place vehicle on blocks. Remove wheel. Remove hairpin-shaped locking rings from guide pins. Pull out one of the lock pins while holding damper springs in place. Remove springs and other lock pin. Remove pads.

Carefully clean out cavity that holds pads. Replace any of the rubber covers that are damaged. If dirt has gotten into cylinder due to damaged cover, brake unit should be reconditioned. To make room for new brake pads, the plungers must be

Removing disc brake pads.

127

pressed into the cylinders. This is facilitated by opening the air vent nipple. Close nipple after pressing in cylinders. Note also that the fluid in the master cylinder may rise and overflow when pressing in cylinders. Prevent fluid from getting on linings or brake disc. Install new pads and one of the lock pins, then damping springs and other lock pin. Install hairpin-shaped locking rings. Check that pads are movable. Press brake pedal several times to check that pedal is operating normally. As a rule bleeding is not required after replacing pads. Replace wheel and check brake fluid level in master cylinder.

Removing rear disc brake caliper.

BRAKE CALIPER REPLACEMENT

Jack up vehicle and place on blocks. Remove wheel. Disconnect brake lines and tape openings to prevent dirt from entering and unnecessary leakage. Remove mounting bolts and brake caliper.

Place new caliper into position. See that contact surfaces are clean and not damaged, since the position of the caliper in relation to the brake disc is very important. Install mounting bolts and check to see that brake disc can rotate easily in the brake pads.

BRAKE DISC REMOVAL

The brake disc should be inspected for wear, run-out and thickness. Run-out must not exceed .004″ for the front wheel brakes and .006″ for the rear, at the outer edge of the disc. See first that wheel bearing adjustment is correct and that disc fits hub securely. Then use micrometer to check run-out of the brake disc. If brake disc is defective, it should be replaced. To do this, first remove brake caliper as described, then remove lock bolts and lift off brake disc. Tap on the inside of the disc several times with a plastic hammer.

Checking disc brake runout.

Drum Brakes

Volvo drum brakes are of conventional design having the front and rear shoes pressed outward against an enclosing drum by a single, two-direction hydraulic cylinder. Equal braking is possible by having the wheel cylinders push the shoes out to initial drum contact with an extremely light pedal pressure. All shoes make contact evenly before full pressure is reached.

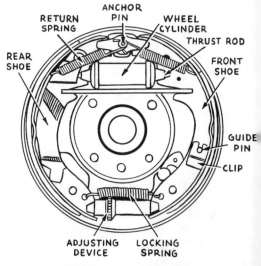

Right rear wheel brake drum.

Brake Shoe Replacement

Remove wheel and drum assembly for access to brake shoes. Disconnect locking spring, pull shoes apart and remove adjusting device. Remove locking clips at the sides.

Turn shoes outward until wheel cylinder thrust rods are released. Then turn shoes inward, release return springs and extract shoes for replacement or relining. If relining brake shoes, drill out lining rivets to avoid shoe rim distortion that punching-out causes. File off burrs around rivet holes. Keep hands clean while handling new linings.

Wheel Cylinder Inspection and Overhaul

Carefully pull lower edges of wheel cylinder boots away from cylinders and note if interior is wet—an indication of brake fluid seepage past the piston cup. If so, cylinder overhaul is required.

Clean dirt from all surrounding surfaces and then disconnect and seal off brake line (tape is often satisfactory for sealing). Remove cylinder from backing plate.

Dismantle boots, pistons, cups and spring from cylinder. Remove bleeder valve. Discard boots and cups; clean other parts with fresh brake fluid. Use no fluid containing even a trace of mineral oil.

Light scratches and corrosion can be polished from pistons and bore with fine emery cloth or steel wool. Dip all parts in brake fluid and reassemble. After installation, adjust brakes and road test for performance.

Brake Drum Inspection

Thoroughly clean and inspect brake drums for cracks, scoring and out-of-round. Polish out slight scores with emery cloth. Shallow grooves can be removed by boring provided oversized linings are obtainable. Out-of-round drums cause excessive wear on other brake parts as well as on tires. Maximum tolerable runout is .006″. Measure for run-out by checking along open and closed edges of machined surface and at right angles.

Before reinstalling brake drum, inspect all brake pipe and hose connections for fluid leakage. Tighten these connections

and apply heavy pressure to brake pedal to recheck seal. Inspect rear wheel backing plate for leaks from wheel bearing oil seals. Replace seals if needed. Check all backing plate bolts for tightness. Clean away all dirt from assemblies and repack wheel bearings.

Master Cylinder

Series 140 Volvos utilize a dual master cylinder and two separate hydraulic circuits, one serving the right rear wheel and the lower set of two cylinders in each front wheel, and the other serving the left rear wheel and the upper set of cylinders in the front wheels. Thus, braking is still maintained even if one of the lines should fail.

Master Cylinder Overhaul

Disconnect and tape brake lines entering master cylinder. Remove mounting nuts and master cylinder, and pour out brake fluid. Hold master cylinder firmly in vise and with both hands lift fluid container up from rubber seals. Remove filler cap and strainer from container, as well as nuts and rubber seals from the cylinder. Remove brake contact and stop screw. Remove lock ring from primary plunger and remove plungers. If second plunger does not shake out, remove by blowing air in the hole for the brake contact.

1. Brake light contact
2. To left brake valve
3. To 6-branch union
4. Brake fluid container
5. To right brake valve
6. To 6-branch union
7. Master cylinder
8. Mounting bolt

Dual master brake cylinder.

Remove two seals from secondary plunger, being careful not to damage the surfaces of the plunger. If reconditioning, the primary plunger should be completely replaced, so it is not necessary to disassemble it. Clean all parts in fresh brake fluid and blow dry with compressed air. Then coat parts with brake fluid for reassembly. Examine cylinder carefully. If there are scores or scratches, cylinder should be replaced. If wear is suspected, measure diameter. Cylinder diameter should not exceed .881″, while plunger diameter should not be less than .870″. In addition to the primary plunger, the secondary plunger seals, the stop screw and washer, the circlip and the rubber seals for the fluid container should also be replaced.

Install plunger with seals and spring after dipping in brake fluid. Insert new primary plunger with washer and circlip. Check to see that hole for stop screw is clear and insert stop screw and sealing washer. Tighten to torque of 9.5 ft. lb. Check movement of plungers and make sure that through-flow holes are clear, including equalizer hole which can be checked with a soft copper, .5 mm diameter wire. If equalizer hole is not clear, master cylinder may be incorrectly assembled. Install container nuts with washers and rubber seals, container and brake contact.

Bleeding Brake System

Whenever any part of the hydraulic brake system has been removed, it is necessary to bleed air that has become trapped in the system. Also air can enter if quantity of fluid is too small, so first make sure the master cylinder is filled.

Connect one end of a bleeder hose to the air vent on the wheel brake unit and submerge the other end of the hose in a clean glass container partially filled with clean brake fluid. While a helper depresses the brake pedal, open the air nipple, and repeat until the brake fluid that flows out is free of air bubbles. Bleed in this order for 140 Series cars: left rear, right front upper nipple, left front upper nipple, right rear, right front inside and outside lower nipples, left front inside and outside lower nipples. Frequently check

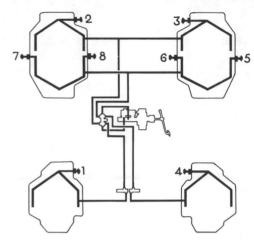

1. Left rear wheel valve
2. Left front wheel upper inner valve
3. Right front wheel, upper inner valve
4. Right rear wheel valve
5. Right front wheel, outer valve
6. Right front wheel, lower inner valve
7. Left front wheel, outer valve
8. Left front wheel, lower inner valve

Hydraulic brake bleeding sequence, series 140 and 164.

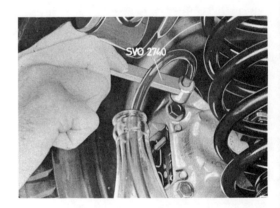

Bleeding left rear brake unit.

level of fluid in master cylinder and fill if low. Do not use fluid bled from system.

Brake Booster

The brake booster available on 140 Series Volvos reduces required foot pressure for braking approximately 25%. The booster is mechanically controlled by the foot pedal and conveys this pressure along with an engine vacuum assistance to the dual master cylinder. A vacuum control valve prevents air from flowing back into booster when engine is not running. The valve must be replaced when defective.

CHECKING BRAKE BOOSTER OPERATION

The operation of the brake booster can be checked easily. With engine off, use up all vacuum by depressing brake pedal several times. Hold pedal down and start engine. As vacuum builds, the pedal will move farther (held under same foot pressure) as power is developed by booster. Check out the booster vacuum system along the hose, at the vacuum valve, and at all connections. Inspect filter for restriction. If the booster is defective, it must be replaced.

BRAKE BOOSTER REPLACEMENT

Remove master cylinder. Disconnect fork at front of booster from brake pedal and disconnect vacuum hose from check valve. Remove four mounting screws from bracket and lift booster cylinder forward.

Loosen lock nut and unscrew fork. Remove rubber cover and thrust rod from cylinder. Assemble in reverse order of above, and bleed the entire brake system.

Brake Specifications

Model	Type		Brake Cyl. Bore (In.)			Drum or Disc Diam. (In.)	
	Front	Rear	Master Cyl.	Wheel Cyl.		Front	Rear
				Front	Rear		
PV444	Drum	Drum					
PV544	Drum	Drum	1	1	.813	9	9
122, P1800	Disc	Drum					
142, 144	Disc	Disc	.882	1.422	1.422	10.7	11.6
145	Disc	Disc	.882	1.422	1.5	10.7	11.6
164	Disc	Disc	.95	1.422	1.422	10.7	11.6

New brake lining thickness is .394 in.

Conversion—Metric and U.S. Measures

Linear Units (Distance, Length, Angle)

1 kilometer = 0.6214 miles or 3,280 feet
1 mile = 1.6093 kilometers
    Multiply kilometers by 0.6214 to get miles.
    Multiply miles by 1.6093 to get kilometers.
1 kilometer = 1000 meters
1 meter = 3.281 feet or 39.370 inches
1 centimeter = 0.394 inches
1 inch = 2.540 centimeters
    Multiply centimeters by 0.394 to get inches.
    Multiply inches by 2.54 to get centimeters.

Cubic Units (Volume, Displacement)

1 liter = 1000 cubic centimeters
1 cubic centimeter (milliliter) = 0.061 cubic inches
1 cubic inch = 16.387 cubic centimeters
    Multiply cubic centimeters by 0.61 to get
    cubic inches. Multiply cubic inches by
    16.387 to get cubic centimeters.
1 liter = 0.264 gallons = 1.057 quarts = 2.1 pints
1 gallon = 3.785 liters = 231 cubic inches
    Multiply liters by 0.264 to get gallons.
    Multiply gallons by 231 to get cubic inches.
Engine displacement—Cubic inch displacement is
    found by multiplying the bore by itself;
    multiplying this answer by 0.7854; multi-
    plying this answer by the stroke; and multi-
    plying this answer by the number of cyl-
    inders.
The constant 0.7854 is used rather than π (the
    mathematical constant, 3.14159) because
    the bore of the cylinder is the diameter,
    not the radius.
Using π, the formula is:

$$\left(\frac{bore}{2}\right)^2 \times \pi \times (stroke) \times (\# \ cylinders)$$
$$= displacement$$

The same formula is used to determine the dis-
    placement of an engine in metric units
    (centimeters), but only after the millimeter
    bore and stroke dimensions are changed to
    centimeters. Change millimeters to centi-
    meters by dividing by ten.

Force Units (Pressure, Torque)

1 atmosphere (atm) = 14.7 pounds per sq. in. (psi)
1 psi = 0.68 atmosphere
    Pressure is measured as force against a
    surface, not volume. A bicycle tire at 50
    psi has far less air in it than a car tire
    having 17 psi.
1 kilogram per sq. centimeter = 14.223 lbs. sq. in.
1 kilogram-meter = 7.233 foot-lbs.
    A foot-pound is a unit of force equal to one
    pound raised one foot. An inch-pound is
    one pound raised one inch.

BRITISH IMPERIAL AND U.S. LIQUID
MEASURES

	Imperial	U.S.
gallon	277.4 (cu. in.)	231 (cu. in.)
quart	69.4	57.8
pint	34.7	28.9

GASOLINE CONSUMPTION (by miles and
kilometers)

1 mile per gallon = 0.355 kilometers per liter
30 miles per gallon = 10.64 kilometers per liter
1 kilometer per liter = 2.82 miles per gallon
8 kilometers per liter = 22.6 miles per gallon

COMMON AUTOMOTIVE ABBREVIATIONS

L	=	liters
mm	=	millimeters
ohv	=	overhead valves
CIH	=	camshaft in cylinder head (rocker arm required)
ohc	=	overhead camshaft (no rocker arm required)
bhp	=	braking horsepower
SAE	=	Society of Automotive Engineers
rpm	=	revolutions per minute
ft.-lbs.	=	foot-pounds (unit of force)
in.-lbs.	=	inch-pounds
POE	=	port of entry

Conversion—Millimeters to Decimal Inches

mm	inches	mm	inches	mm	inches	mm	inches	mm	inches
1	.039 370	31	1.220 470	61	2.401 570	91	3.582 670	210	8.267 700
2	.078 740	32	1.259 840	62	2.440 940	92	3.622 040	220	8.661 400
3	.118 110	33	1.299 210	63	2.480 310	93	3.661 410	230	9.055 100
4	.157 480	34	1.338 580	64	2.519 680	94	3.700 780	240	9.448 800
5	.196 850	35	1.377 949	65	2.559 050	95	3.740 150	250	9.842 500
6	.236 220	36	1.417 319	66	2.598 420	96	3.779 520	260	10.236 200
7	.275 590	37	1.456 689	67	2.637 790	97	3.818 890	270	10.629 900
8	.314 960	38	1.496 050	68	2.677 160	98	3.858 260	280	11.032 600
9	.354 330	39	1.535 430	69	2.716 530	99	3.897 630	290	11.417 300
10	.393 700	40	1.574 800	70	2.755 900	100	3.937 000	300	11.811 000
11	.433 070	41	1.614 170	71	2.795 270	105	4.133 848	310	12.204 700
12	.472 440	42	1.653 540	72	2.834 640	110	4.330 700	320	12.598 400
13	.511 810	43	1.692 910	73	2.874 010	115	4.527 550	330	12.992 100
14	.551 180	44	1.732 280	74	2.913 380	120	4.724 400	340	13.385 800
15	.590 550	45	1.771 650	75	2.952 750	125	4.921 250	350	13.779 500
16	.629 920	46	1.811 020	76	2.992 120	130	5.118 100	360	14.173 200
17	.669 290	47	1.850 390	77	3.031 490	135	5.314 950	370	14.566 900
18	.708 660	48	1.889 760	78	3.070 860	140	5.511 800	380	14.960 600
19	.748 030	49	1.929 130	79	3.110 230	145	5.708 650	390	15.354 300
20	.787 400	50	1.968 500	80	3.149 600	150	5.905 500	400	15.748 000
21	.826 770	51	2.007 870	81	3.188 970	155	6.102 350	500	19.685 000
22	.866 140	52	2.047 240	82	3.228 340	160	6.299 200	600	23.622 000
23	.905 510	53	2.086 610	83	3.267 710	165	6.496 050	700	27.559 000
24	.944 880	54	2.125 980	84	3.307 080	170	6.692 900	800	31.496 000
25	.984 250	55	2.165 350	85	3.346 450	175	6.889 750	900	35.433 000
26	1.023 620	56	2.204 720	86	3.385 820	180	7.086 600	1000	39.370 000
27	1.062 990	57	2.244 090	87	3.425 190	185	7.283 450	2000	78.740 000
28	1.102 360	58	2.283 460	88	3.464 560	190	7.480 300	3000	118.110 000
29	1.141 730	59	2.322 830	89	3.503 903	195	7.677 150	4000	157.480 000
30	1.181 100	60	2.362 200	90	3.543 300	200	7.874 000	5000	196.850 000

To change decimal millimeters to decimal inches, position the decimal point where desired on either side of the millimeter measurement shown and reset the inches decimal by the same number of digits in the same direction. For example, to convert .001 mm into decimal inches, reset the decimal behind the 1 mm (shown on the chart) to .001; change the decimal inch equivalent (.039″ shown) to .00039″).

Conversion—Common Fractions to Decimals and Millimeters

Common Fractions	Decimal Fractions	Millimeters (approx.)	Common Fractions	Decimal Fractions	Millimeters (approx.)	Common Fractions	Decimal Fractions	Millimeters (approx.)
1/128	.008	0.20	11/32	.344	8.73	43/64	.672	17.07
1/64	.016	0.40	23/64	.359	9.13	11/16	.688	17.46
1/32	.031	0.79	3/8	.375	9.53	45/64	.703	17.86
3/64	.047	1.19	25/64	.391	9.92	23/32	.719	18.26
1/16	.063	1.59	13/32	.406	10.32	47/64	.734	18.65
5/64	.078	1.98	27/64	.422	10.72	3/4	.750	19.05
3/32	.094	2.38	7/16	.438	11.11	49/64	.766	19.45
7/64	.109	2.78	29/64	.453	11.51	25/32	.781	19.84
1/8	.125	3.18	15/32	.469	11.91	51/64	.797	20.24
9/64	.141	3.57	31/64	.484	12.30	13/16	.813	20.64
5/32	.156	3.97	1/2	.500	12.70	53/64	.828	21.03
11/64	.172	4.37	33/64	.516	13.10	27/32	.844	21.43
3/16	.188	4.76	17/32	.531	13.49	55/64	.859	21.83
13/64	.203	5.16	35/64	.547	13.89	7/8	.875	22.23
7/32	.219	5.56	9/16	.563	14.29	57/64	.891	22.62
15/64	.234	5.95	37/64	.578	14.68	29/32	.906	23.02
1/4	.250	6.35	19/32	.594	15.08	59/64	.922	23.42
17/64	.266	6.75	39/64	.609	15.48	15/16	.938	23.81
9/32	.281	7.14	5/8	.625	15.88	61/64	.953	24.21
19/64	.297	7.54	41/64	.641	16.27	31/32	.969	24.61
5/16	.313	7.94	21/32	.656	16.67	63/64	.984	25.00
21/64	.328	8.33						

Automotive Parts Terminology

In some cases there is more than one name for an automobile part or assembly. Equivalent meanings are given below. "Br" stands for British.

CARBURETOR

air correction jet (Br), high speed air bleed
butterfly, throttle valve, throttle plate
choke tube (Br), venturi
emulsion tube (Br), main vent tube
idle speed screw, throttle stop screw
main jet (Br), main metering jet
pilot jet (Br), idling jet
pilot jet air bleed (Br), idle air adjusting screw
progression circuit (Br), second idle stage
slow-running adjustment (Br), idle speed adjustment
slow-running volume adjustment (Br), idle mixture adjustment
strangler (Br), choke

ENGINE

bearing insert, bearing shell, bearing
core plug (Br), welsh plug, drain plug
crankpin, journal

gudgeon pin (Br), piston pin, wrist pin
retaining clip, circlip, snapring
scraper ring, oil ring
clutch driven plate, drive disc
oil sump, oil pan
slave cylinder, servo cylinder, operating cylinder

ELECTRICAL

alternator, AC generator
dynamo, generator
earth, ground
distributor shaft, driving spindle

SUSPENSION

king pin slant, steering knuckle inclination, swivel axle
control arm, control link, wishbone
cross member, assembly member

MISCELLANEOUS

filling up, topping up
bushings, bushes, shell bearings
fork, yoke
brake backing plate, securing plate
spanner, wrench

Miscellaneous Specifications

Specification	B-16	B-18	B-20	B-30
Maximum Flywheel runout (in) @ diam. (in.)	.008	.002 @ 5.90	.002 @ 5.90	.002 @ .5.90
Camshaft Bearing Clear. (in.)	.0010-.0029	.0008-.0030	.0008-.0030	.0008-.0030
Camshaft end-play (in.)	–	.0008-.0024	.0008-.0024	.0008-.0024
Timing gear backlash (in)	.0004-.0016	.0016-.0032	.0016-.0032	.0016-.0032
Timing gear tooth flank clear. (in.)	–	.0016-.0032	–	–
Oil Pump Gear end-play (in)	.0008-.0040	.0008-.0040	.0008-.0040	.0008-.0040
Oil Pump Gear Backlash (in.)	.006-.014	.006-.014	.006-.014	.006-.014
Oil Press. Relief spring free lgth. (in)	1.22	1.22	1.54	1.54
Rear Axle Ratio	–	4.10:1 or 4.56:1	4.10:1 or 4.30:1	3.31:1 or 3.73:1
Rear Axle Gear Backlash (in.)	–	.004-.008	.004-.008	.005-.008
Rear Axle [1] Pinion Preload (in/lb)	–	9.55-20	9.55-20	9.55-20
Differential Bearing Preload (in.)	–	.005-.008	.005-.008	.005-.008

[1] New bearings.